Guide to the
Whiskies
of Scotland

DEREK COOPER

Series Editor
Pamela Vandyke Price

PITMAN

PITMAN PUBLISHING LIMITED
39 Parker Street, London WC2B 5PB

Associated Companies
Copp Clark Ltd, Toronto
Fearon-Pitman Publishers Inc, Belmont, California
Pitman Publishing Co. SA (Pty) Ltd, Johannesburg
Pitman Publishing New Zealand Ltd, Wellington
Pitman Publishing Pty Ltd, Melbourne

© Derek Cooper, 1978
First published in Great Britain 1978

Text set in 10/11 pt Baskerville, by Carlinpoint Ltd
and printed by photolithography at Billing & Sons Ltd, Guildford, London and
Worcester

ISBN 0 273 01254 1

Also in this series:

Acknowledgements

I would like to thank all those members of the whisky industry who went out of their way to show me their distilleries, maltings, warehouses and blending plants and share with me their expertise, enthusiasm and knowledge, including:

Ian Allen, George Ballingall, Adam Bergius, John Burns, G. G. Carmichael, Trevor Cowan, Charles Craig, David Crockett, Gardner Ferrier, Ian Fletcher, David Grant, L. A. H. Harvey, David Heilbron, Ian Henderson, Dr J. E. Jackson, R. Stuart Lang, A. M. Lawson, F. Douglas Lemkes, James Logan, Bruce Lundee, David Macdonald, Gordon MacIntosh, Ian Mackenzie, Dr K. G. Mackenzie, Donald Mackinlay, Michael Martin, Willie Meikle, Denis Nicol, Stuart Robertson, Neil Shaw, P. G. Shiach, Brian Spiller, and Iain Tennant.

I was greatly helped by the information and background material supplied by: Lang Brothers, The Invergordon Distillers, Charles Mackinlay & Co., Macdonald & Muir, North British Grain Distillery, Long John International and Long John Distilleries, White Horse Distillers, Arthur Bell & Sons, James Buchanan & Co., Findlater (Scotch Whisky), William Grant & Sons, John Haig and Co., Macallan-Glenlivet, Chas. Mackinlay & Co., James Martin & Co., Stanley P. Morrison, Geo. & G. J. Smith, Wm Teacher & Sons, Waverley Vintners, The Distillers Company Limited, Whyte & Mackay Distillers, Justerini & Brooks and Scottish Grain Distillers.

I am also greatly indebted to Jeffrey Wormstone of the Scotch Whisky Association and Graham Smith, Librarian and Archivist, H. M. Customs and Excise for their help and assistance; to Jean Hodge who came from Aberdeen to type my manuscript and to Bill Smith of Wm. Grants who very kindly distilled out some of its imperfections: born at Cragganmore where his father was 'brewer', brought up at Royal Lochnagar which his father managed, and with a lifetime spent in the industry, few know more about *uisge beatha*.

Derek Cooper
Portree, Isle of Skye
July 1978

Contents

APPENDIXES

Glenturret distillery, Crieff

Scotch Whisky Defined

Whisky is made all over the world from New Zealand to Finland and nowhere more assiduously than in Japan. But Scotch whisky can only be made in Scotland. Had anyone sought a definition of Scotch whisky in 1905 it would, much to the delight of the traditional distillers, who made their malt whisky from malted barley in pot stills, have excluded the grain whisky made in patent stills from maize and barley.

In November of that year a London magistrate ruled that a shopkeeper had contravened Section 6 of the Food and Drugs Act of 1875 by selling a patent still whisky to someone who had asked for Scotch.

The magistrate decided that the whisky — ninety per cent the product of a patent still, and ten per cent pot still — was not legally entitled to be called Scotch whisky.

Now this was a decision which pleased the malt distillers but dismayed the grain distillers, in particular the all-powerful and recently established D.C.L.*. There was an appeal to Quarter Sessions but the bench was divided and no decision was reached.

It was obviously in the interests of both pot and patent distillers that the product should be legally defined; the former were confident that the description 'Scotch' could only be applied to their product; the latter were hopeful that however whisky was made, if it was made in Scotland it should by law be able to call itself 'Scotch'.

In 1908 the Prime Minister appointed a Royal Commission to resolve the deadlock and both parties submitted evidence. With hindsight it is clear that neither malt whisky nor grain on their own could have produced the massive sales which blends enjoy

* The Distillers Company Limited, which today owns 31 per cent of the Scotch whisky industry, began life in 1877 when six grain distillers amalgamated 'to secure the benefits of reduced expenses and increased profits'.

today. The blenders had evolved a drink which the public had come to enjoy — something which could be full and authoritative with a preponderance of malts or light and bland with a preponderance of grain.

But the 134 pot distillers, who regarded grain whisky as a neutral spirit incapable of improving with age, a dumb and silent spirit unfit to share a bottle with such triumphant tenors as Glenlivet or great basses like Lagavulin, did not see it in this light at all.

They were doomed to disappointment. The Royal Commission found that both patent still and pot still whisky were entitled to be called Scotch and their historic statement cleared the road for the powerful grain distillers and blenders to buy out many a small malt distillery. The future of Scotch was defined in these words:

'Whiskey* is a spirit obtained by distillation from a mash of cereal grains saccharified by the diastase of malt; "Scotch" whiskey is whiskey, as above defined, distilled in Scotland; and "Irish" whiskey is whiskey, as above defined, distilled in Ireland.'

It was a verdict which outraged the later purists: 'The tasteless distillate of grain, made at one process in a patent still, is now equally entitled to call itself whisky as the exquisite, pot-still, malt whisky, dried above a peat fire,' lamented Aeneas Macdonald.

Neil Gunn, former Exciseman and Highland author, waxed sad and lyrical: 'A fine pot-still whisky is as noble a product of Scotland as any burgundy or champagne is of France. We have the most perfect whisky in the world. What are we doing about it? Hauling down the red lion on its golden field and hoisting in place thereof Red Biddy on a field sable.'

But things didn't turn out so badly after all. There are now blends enough for all tastes from the most bland and light to the mellowed delights of a really well aged and harmoniously composed blend and never before have so many single malt whiskies been so widely available.

The Problem of Proof

'Proof' is a method of describing how strong a whisky is — in other words how much alcohol there is in the water. Since alcohol catches fire easily (as any waiter in an expense account restaurant will demonstrate at the faintest cry of *Crêpes Suzette*) the simplest and earliest method of measuring the alcohol content of a liquid was burning it off and measuring the volume of water left behind.

A more colourful test was to mix the spirit under scrutiny with

---

* Whisky was spelt with or without a final 'e' fairly indiscriminately until recent times. Today 'whisky' refers to the spirit distilled in Scotland, 'whiskey' is distilled in Ireland.

gunpowder and put a taper to it. If it exploded it was *over proof*; if it ignited and gave off a steady flame it was *proof*; if it failed to burn it was *under proof*. Another method was to shake a quantity of whisky in a bottle and note the manifestation of bubbles. It's an experiment you can perform easily for yourself: next time you're in a bar with a good display of malts ask the barman to let you shake a bottle of 70 and a bottle of 105 proof — the stronger malt will produce more bubbles than the weaker.

In the eighteenth century the proof of a spirit for most drinkers lay in its power to bowl you over — they weren't concerned with precise measurements. But the Excise men were. They used hydrometers (Boyle's at first and then in 1787 Clarke's improved version) but these were far from accurate. In 1802 a Committee of Enquiry was appointed to produce if possible a reliable measurement of proof. They examined various devices presented to them by members of the public and finally chose a hydrometer (an instrument which measures the density of liquids and hence their strength) offered by an Exciseman called Bartholomew Sikes. The Sikes hydrometer is still in use today and proof spirit in Britain is defined by Sikes as a mixture of 57.1 per cent of alcohol and 42.9 per cent water. In the United States, proof spirit is fifty per cent alcohol, fifty per cent water.

The different strengths of proof are expressed in degrees and blended whisky is normally sold in Britain at 70° or 30 under proof — proof being taken as 100. Until World War One Scotch was normally sold at 25 degrees under proof (75°) but with grain in short supply the industry was ordered to weaken its whisky to 30 under proof (70°). This was a wartime economy measure to which they have adhered patriotically ever since.

Blends are still exported to the United States at 75° Sikes, which corresponds to 86.8° proof measured by the American system. Other countries use other systems.

On 1st January 1980, however, the old methods are to be replaced in all countries which subscribe to the International Organisation of Legal Metrology (OIML), by much simpler and more logical methods of measuring the alcoholic strength of liquids.

The 162-year reign of Sikes will give way to a system of measurement in terms of percentage of alcohol by volume at 20°C. From that date the OIML system will be the only one permitted within the E.E.C. and quantities will be measured in hectolitres, litres, centilitres and the conversion will be based on 1 gallon being equal to 4.5609 litres.

Alas, I'm too innumerate for all this and just as I still think of a really hot day as being 80 in the shade I shall go on thinking of a good strength for malt as 80 in the bottle. But for more forward-looking and accommodating folk here is a comparative table for the old Sikes and the new metric system, which is also likely to be adopted by the USA, USSR, Japan and the former dependencies of the colonial powers.

Sikes	OIML
65.5	37.4
70	39.9
75	42.8
80	45.6
100	57.1
106	60.5
111	63.3
115	65.6
120	68.5

Whisky, gin, vodka and rum are generally 40 per cent by volume on the OIML Scale; other alcoholic drinks are not so strong.

Wash and low wines stills

Scotch in History

Scotland derives its name from the Irish Gaelic tribe which migrated to the western islands and Argyll in the fifth century AD. It derived its Christianity from an Irishman too: a remarkable saint called Columba who stepped ashore on the island of Iona in the year 563. And there's good reason to believe that the knowledge that barley could be metamorphosed into *uisge beatha,* the water of life, came over the sea from Ireland as well.

But just as the Scots distilled their religion into the unique and unyielding spirit of Presbyterianism, so over the years they have evolved a unique liquid spirit which has never been reproduced anywhere else in the world. Technicians have tried to make it in Finland, Portugal and New Zealand but an arcane alchemy which refuses to yield to analysis always defeats them. Only in Scotland can Scotch whisky be made. As a Highland distiller told me with some modesty: 'we know what we're doing right enough, but we're still not sure what really goes on inside the still.' Japanese chemists come frequently to the Scottish glens; they peer intently and bear samples away to their laboratories but they've never found out what strange mystery occurs in the Spey valley and on the shores of Islay that cannot be re-enacted in Osaka or Tokyo.

Whether it was Irish monks who brought the art of distilling to Scotland or not, whisky certainly had a respectable and holy origin. Sixteen years before the monks of Fécamp started producing Bénédictine the Scottish Exchequer Rolls of 1494 recorded the provision of 'eight bolls of malt to Friar John Cor wherewith to make aquavitae', but distilling must have been going on long before that. The heady concocting of intoxicating water from grape and grain is almost as old as cultivation itself. Semantically it surfaces in French as *eau de vie,* in Danish as *akvavit,* in Erse as *usquebaugh* and in Gaelic as *uisge beatha.* Gradually the soft-vowelled sound *ooska* became on Anglo-Saxon tongues *ooskie* and eventually whisky.

It had many variations. Indeed the *usquebaugh* produced in

Ireland frequently contained aromatic spices like mace, cloves, cinnamon, coriander and saffron. Perhaps that is why Dr. Johnson defined *usquebaugh* as 'a compound distilled spirit, being drawn on aromaticks' and was less specific about the Scottish equivalent apart from noting that 'it is somewhat better.' Johnson didn't taste it until he was on the last lap of his famous Hebridean jaunt in 1773. In Edinburgh and the islands he and Boswell had been offered brandy and wine but never the native *uisge*. At last on crossing from Mull to the mainland they reached Inveraray and there at the inn Johnson was in an experimental mood. 'Come', he said, 'let me know what it is that makes a Scotsman happy.' Having drunk it all but the last drop which, recorded Boswell, 'I begged leave to pour into my glass that I might say we had drank whisky together', Johnson pronounced it 'preferable to any English malt brandy' but never tasted it again.

A Sovereign Liquor

Because spirits, in the medieval pharmacopoeia, were regarded as a nostrum for many ailments and debilities, the Edinburgh authorities decreed in 1505 that only surgeons and barbers could sell them. This was the beginning of a series of unpopular laws that either limited the sale of whisky or imposed taxes on its production. As the restriction grew, a do-it-yourself movement was born: whisky, distilled illicitly, became at once a form of currency (more valuable and portable than a sack of barley), a consolation and an efficacious medicine.

In 1578 Holinshed published the seminal *Chronicles of England, Scotland and Ireland* which Shakespeare was to mine so successfully a few years later. The *Chronicles* contained a short dissertation on *uisge beatha* and a testimonial which has never been surpassed even by contemporary practitioners of the black art of advertising:

> Beying moderatelie taken, it sloweth age; it strengthened youthe; it helpeth digestion; it cutteth fleume; it abandoneth melancholie; it relisheth the harte; it lighteneth the mynde; it quickeneth the spirites; it cureth the hydropsis; it healeth the stranguary; it preserveth the head from whyrling — the eyes from dazelying — the tongue from lispying — the mouth from snafflying — the teethe from chatteryng — the throte from ratlyng — the weasan from stieflying — the stomach from wamblyng — the harte from swellyng — the bellie from wirthchyng — the guts from rumblyng — the hands from shiveryng — the sinowes from shrinkyng — the veynes from crumplyng — the bones from soakyng — trulie it is a soverainge liquor if it be orderlie taken.

It was the kind of medicine that put you on your feet from the start: 'A man of the Hebrides,' Johnson observed while in Skye, 'as soon as he appears in the morning swallows a glass of whisky: yet they are not a drunken race, at least I was never present at much intemperance; but no man is so abstemious as to refuse the morning dram which they call a skalk.'

Martin Martin, tutor to the Macleods of Skye at the end of the seventeenth century, noted that the Hebrideans commonly used strong liquor as a specific against the climate 'by which they fancy that they qualify the Moisture of the Air.' In 1771 Smollett referred to its therapeutic qualities in *Humphrey Clinker.* The Scots, he said, were used to it from the cradle 'and find it an excellent preservative against the winter cold, which must be extreme on these mountains. I am told that it is given with great success to infants, as a cordial in the confluent smallpox when that eruption seems to flag.'

And whisky had its terminal role as well. On the fateful field of Culloden in 1745 Holy Eucharist was administered to the dying Lord Strathallan 'with oat-cake and whisky, the requisite elements being not obtainable.' After death too whisky played a leading part in the funerary proceedings. When Flora Macdonald, protectress of Bonnie Prince Charlie, was laid to rest in her native Kilmuir, three thousand mourners gathered to lament her passing — and drowned their grief in 300 gallons of whisky. At the funeral of the Hon. Alexander Fraser of Lovat a few years later, several of the hearse bearers, unbalanced by grief and whisky, fell into the grave; brawls, mayhem and even violent death were not uncommon at a really convivial interment.

Although the Danes had a horrifying reputation for imbibing akvavit, the Highlanders seldom lagged behind. In 1588 Frederik II of Denmark drank himself to death, and Shakespeare's portrait of court life at Elsinore would have been appreciated by the Jacobeans; after a carousing state visit from King Christian the Londoners delightedly renamed the Magpie and Stump tavern, near the Old Bailey, the King of Denmark. But when Christian's sister Anne, who married King James VI of Scotland, introduced to London a Danish courtier who had outdrunk every nobleman in Europe he was finally seen under the table after a three day boozing bout by Sir Robert Lawrie, a Scot 'unmatched at the bottle, unconquered in war.'

The Age of Smuggling

The gradual increase of Excise duty on spirits only served to spur the people on to new and more frenzied smuggling. The hard stuff, in the shape of brandy and gin, was brought in from Europe and every community had its smugglers — a term which was used to cover not only the importers of duty free liquor but the distillers of the native Highland dew.

In the eighteenth century the Highlands of Scotland were very much a *terra incognita*. Although Captain Cook had by then charted the New Hebrides in the South Seas, large parts of the far north of Scotland remained not only uncharted but largely unvisited. The Act of Union with England in 1707 had given English revenue officers the power on paper to tax the production of whisky but not the means.

It was the failure of the Jacobite cause in 1715 that opened up the Highlands; orders from London despatched General Wade north to build strongholds throughout the Highlands and link them with a network of military roads. The roads are there to this day, some still in use, some overgrown; and names like Fort George, Fort William and Fort Augustus still commemorate the Hanoverian determination to crush the rebellious clans.

There was a second and final rising in 1745 and after Bonnie Prince Charlie's defeat at Culloden the avenging English Redcoats were sent to ravage the land. The Gaelic language was proscribed, the lairds were humbled into mere landlords and the power and the glory of the clan chiefs were dissipated in the gaming rooms and watering places of the soft south.

The English ascendancy was established and there was a following wave of legislation designed to subdue the defiant North. When Boswell and Johnson passed through Edinburgh in August 1773, eight licensed distilleries were contributing in a small way to the revenue of the United Kingdom. But there were, it was thought, nearly 400 unregistered stills contributing only to the personal support of the freebooters who ran them.

A long battle ensued between the Excise men, or gaugers* as they were known, and the operators of clandestine stills, for whom the Excise laws were alien both in their language and their inhibiting intent.

Smuggling became as much a part of agricultural life as ploughing and haymaking. Around Glenlivet and Tomintoul alone, blessed with abundant burns and peat there for the cutting, 200 illicit stills were operating. Barley was turned into whisky, which was then exchanged for money to pay the rent and buy the seed for more barley.

In Lewis the tacksmen† went so far as to provide their tenants with grain so that they could convert it into liquid currency which once re-collected could be disposed of profitably. Everyone from the highest to the lowest was involved in smuggling even if they were only at the receiving end.

'Even so late as then,' wrote Dr. John Mackenzie of Inverewe, referring to the 1820s, 'one would go a long way before one met a person who shrank from smuggling. My father never tasted any but smuggled whisky and when every mortal that called for him

* They gauged the contents of casks.

† Men who leased a large piece or 'tack' of land from the proprietor of an estate and then sublet it as small farms.

had a dram instantly poured into him the ankers* of whisky emptied yearly must have been numerous indeed.' The native Highlander regarded the Excise laws as iniquitous and Mackenzie recalled the Dean of Ross and Argyll looking sorrowfully back 'on the happy times when he was young and his father distilled every Saturday what was needed for the following week.'

Ironically it was the invidious way in which the duty was raised on the whisky produced in the legal distilleries in the Lowlands which gave the homemade Highland whisky its superior reputation. In order to avoid the pernicious Malt Tax of 1725 the Lowland distillers mixed unmalted grain with malted barley, sacrificing quality for quantity.

Robert Burns, a poet all his life and Exciseman for a brief part of it, described Lowland whisky as 'a most rascally liquor: and by consequence only drank by the most rascally part of the inhabitants.' (This was the spirit which when exported to England was rectified into gin.) No wonder that George IV and his court preferred the illegal product of the Highland pot stills and that in the words of the geologist and traveller John Macculloch 'the people forbore to purchase at a higher price that which is as nauseous as it is poisonous.' Like many of his contemporaries, Macculloch questioned the long term effects of Excise legislation: 'To make a triple attack on the pocket, the stomach and the constitution at once, argues no very great proficiency in the art by which wealth may be extracted from the people.'

Macculloch, like many visitors to the remoter parts of the Highlands and Islands, was well aware not only of the importance that illicit distilling played in daily life but also its cheap and cheering properties. 'I should be deficient in gratitude to worthy Sir John Barleycorn,' he wrote in 1821, 'if I had not bestowed a few words on him who has so often been a friend of the wet and the weary, who has smoothed the rude path over the mountains, and levelled the boisterous waves of the Western Ocean.'

He had a better chance than any other traveller in the early nineteenth century to watch the battle between the gaugers and their quarry, because he went from island to island in a revenue cutter placed at his disposal by the government. Every now and again they would see the tell-tale smoke on the shore which might be someone innocently burning kelp or less innocently distilling a drop of *uisge beatha*.

The Worm in the Heather

The favoured spots were inland, in the remotest glens which could not be easily reached on foot. In the Islands (and at that time Arran was considered to be 'the Burgundy of all the

---

* a cask holding about eight gallons.

vintages') smugglers often sited their stills on the seashore at the mouth of a burn where they could see a hostile sail a long way off., You might have to abandon the wash* but you could escape with the equipment and live to distil another day.

The key to the whole operation was the worm, the piece of coiled copper tube through which the vapours from the wash-still were condensed. Not infrequently when a worm was worn beyond all use its whereabouts could be revealed to the Excisemen and a reward of £5 collected for disclosing evidence of illicit distillation. With the £5 you could buy yourself a new and better worm!

The government's efforts to wipe out smuggling failed almost everywhere. As a disgruntled Lowland distiller bankrupted by heavy duty and unbridled competition from smugglers told the 1798 Parliamentary Committee: 'the distillery is in a thousand hands. It is not confined to great towns or to regular manufacturers, but spreads itself over the whole face of the country, and in every island from the Orkneys to Jura. There are many who practise this art who are ignorant of every other, and there are distillers who boast that they make the best possible Whiskey who cannot read or write.'

Distilling in the Blood

By the 1820s more than half the whisky drunk in Scotland had been swallowed painlessly without benefit of duty and this despite the fact that as many as 14,000 stills were being confiscated every year. It was apparent that distilling not only quickened a Highlander's pulse, it was a corpuscular part of his blood.

In those early days, large scale distillation was a very hit-and-miss affair; the results were often coarse and harsh. No matter where the spirit was produced, whether in England, Scotland or Ireland, it had to be rectified (redistilled with added drugs and flavouring materials) before consumption. The only genuine whisky which an Englishman could get was the unrectified illicit spirit. Many of the Lowland distilleries were using rye and wheat as well as barley in their mashes and no doubt rectification improved them, but they would have born little relation to the pure malt whisky distilled in the hills of Perth and the valleys of Tay, the Dee and the Don. So the enthusiasm of the Highland smugglers was not as mercenary as the revenue men might have thought; no one in the whole kingdom was making a product to equal theirs.

There were other considerations which made illicit distilling an even more attractive proposition at the beginning of the nineteenth century than it ever had been before — a whole string of new laws which incensed the Scots so much that it became

* A glossary of terms used in the manufacture of whisky will be found in Appendix 4.

almost a point of honour to distil and be damned; a defiance which Burns crystallised in five echoing words — 'Freedom an' whisky gang thegither.'

The Move to Legality

The 1814 law which prohibited the licensing of any still smaller than 500 gallons served only to stoke the peat fires in the distilling glens north of Edinburgh. The anger of the legally licensed Lowland distillers and the pressure on Scottish landowners to restrain their farming tenants from so openly flouting the law eventually prompted a suggestion from the Duke of Gordon, on whose extensive acres the finest whisky in Scotland was being illicitly produced.

He proposed in the House of Lords that if the government would change the tax laws and make it profitable to manufacture legally a whisky which could match the quality of the illicit product, then he and his fellow landowners would do everything they could to put an end to illicit distilling.

The Government welcomed the idea. As well as the excellent Highland whisky which was being smuggled into England in increasing quantities there was also a large-scale production of spurious contraband whiskies made of rye and wheat. A Royal Commission was appointed and in 1823 an Act was passed which sanctioned the distilling of whisky in return for a licence fee of £10 and the payment of 2s 3d per gallon of proof spirit.

This notable piece of legislation founded the whisky industry as we know it today. In the following year the first licence was taken out by a farmer called George Smith of Upper Drumin in Glenlivet. Regarded as a blackleg by the other distillers in the Glenlivet area, Smith was presented with a pair of hair-trigger pistols by the Laird of Aberlour to protect himself against local wrath.

A newly licensed distillery was burnt down by angry smugglers on Deeside and three distillers who bought licences in Glenlivet were quickly forced to shut up shop. But George Smith and farmers like him were not deterred. Within two years the amount of duty-paid whisky had risen from two million gallons to six million gallons. Although illicit stills continued to bubble for domestic consumption, commercial trade gradually passed into the hands of full-time legal distillers. Smith's own malt, *The* Glenlivet, is still revered to this day.

Ten years after the passing of the Act, revenue officers were detecting only two illegal stills a week. By 1864 they recorded less than two a month; by 1874, less than two a quarter.

I have met a Highlander who remembers as a child being taken to a revered place where there had been a worm in the heather but nobody has ever offered me a dram of illicit *uisge*. And yet in

Connemara today it's estimated that some 200 amateurs are actively engaged in fabricating Ireland's *poitin* — a cottage industry worth at a conservative estimate £2 million a year. Surely there must be one Scot with smugglers' blood still pulsing in his veins?

Even if the freebooting spirit waned more quickly in Scotland than it did in Ireland, its gutsy enterprise can be tasted to this day. As that splendid traveller Alfred Barnard observed when he made his epic tour of the Scottish and Irish distilleries in the 1880s: 'no men understood better the localities where they could turn out good spirits, and this fact may be seen to this day, when we find many of the oldest distilleries existing upon sites which have been well-known to have been chosen by smugglers of old as places where the purest mountain streams, flowing over moss and peats, could be used to distil and produce spirits of the finest description.'

An eighteenth-century illicit distillery at work,
with a party of police on its way to seize it

The Making of Malt Whisky

I find it tempting to make analogies between distilleries and vineyards. Just as in Bordeaux there are some vineyards classified as *premier cru*, some as *cru bourgeois*, so most lovers of malt whisky could arrange their favourites in a descending order of merit. Indeed when a few years ago the wine-shipping firm of Lebégue took over the marketing of a distinguished Highland malt made in the Glenlivet area they were tempted, unwisely perhaps, to compare it with a great French wine. 'We can liken this district's fame to that of the Côte d'Or wine area compared with the Midi. We would place Aberlour at the same level as the wines of the Romanée-Conti.'

In grape-growing areas there are the variables of soil and sun, climate and the expertise of the individual winemakers. In Scotland there are other imponderables: the quality of the water, the malting and peating of the barley, the size and shape of the still, the skill of the stillman and the years of maturation.

And just as one vineyard, for reasons that cannot be fully analysed, may produce consistently better wine than a neighbouring vineyard, so distilleries within sight of each other may produce remarkably differing malts. As Maurice Walsh, an Exciseman who took to writing romantic novels in the 1920s put it: 'I knew one small town with seven distilleries and I knew an expert who could distinguish the seven by bouquet alone. The seven distilleries were in one mile of Highland river; they used the same water, peat and malt, and the methods of brewing and distillation were identical, yet each spirit had its own individual bouquet. One, the best, mellowed perfectly in seven years; another, the least good, not a hundred yards away, was still liquid fire at the end of ten years.'

He was talking of the traditional whiskies, made by two separate distillations in a pot still. Unlike grain whisky, which is made largely in towns, most malt distilleries lie in the countryside, many of them in regions of great natural beauty.

Where the Distilleries Are

There are, as we have seen, historic and practical reasons why the early distilleries were built in unpopulated glens and on the shores of remote lochs; in the days of smuggling, out of sight was out of the gauger's eye. Although it helped to be reasonably near a source of barley and peat, these could always be carried over the hills; what was absolutely essential was a supply of clear water not only for soaking the barley and making the mash but for condensing the spirit. So every distillery is either on the banks of a river or burn or on the site of a well or spring. Some distilleries bring their water by pipe from a high-lying loch but wherever the source it must be cold, unpolluted and as constantly flowing as possible.

Many distilleries rely to this day on the same source of water as the old smugglers used in their carefully concealed and primitive bothies.* Over the years although the whiskies themselves may have become lighter, reflecting changing tastes, the basic technique and skills remain substantially the same. A hundred years ago one would have gone by horse and trap to visit a distillery that was driven by water-power or primitive steam machinery. Alongside might well be a farm growing the barley and the peat would be cut nearby. Today, you arrive by car and you will probably discover that the barley has been malted and peat-dried fifty or more miles away, the stills are oil- or gas-fired and the still house controlled from an electronic console. What used to be done laboriously by hand is now accomplished mechanically.

So how much of the traditional artistry and skill can be left? I find the industry divided on this point. If you go into one of the semi-automated distilleries like Caol Ila on Islay or Auchroisk at Mulben you may certainly wonder where the skill comes in; it looks at first sight as if the whisky is being produced by a man pushing buttons. According to an old friend of mine you could take anyone off the street and in three weeks train him to run a modern still house.

'In the old days you'd see a stillman sitting at his still and feeding it with coal, almost by the lump. You'd see him go and put his ear to the still and listen to how it was coming on. And he'd coax the heat gently until the thing was just at the right temperature and the spirit would start coming off nice and gently, no sudden surges. Now its all done by steam; where's the skill?'

But even if technology has made life easier, ironing out the uncertainties, shortening the odds against failure, whisky men are not happy to admit that what they do can be done just by anyone.

* small shelters, usually built of stone and roofed with turf.

Stills and Equipment

Whisky distilling remains a very conservative and traditional craft. When Alfred Barnard visited Laphroaig in the 1880s he was told that the demand for this oily and pungent whisky far exceeded the modest annual output of 24,000 gallons but 'notwithstanding this circumstance, the distiller will not increase the size of the plant, nor enlarge the vessels, lest he should in any way alter the character of this highly prized spirit.'

Among the old generation of distillers, this conservatism extends to the copper stills themselves, which are repaired and patched until their useful life is over. When a new one has to be fashioned as a last resort, the coppersmith reproduces faithfully the contours of the old one — even, so it's said, down to the minutest and coincidental dents.

The oldest method of heating a still was to light a peat, coal or coke fire under it and boil it as you would a giant kettle. Nowadays solid fuelled fires are fed mechanically or butane gas or oil is used. More and more distilleries have been converted to steam heating — coils are placed inside the still itself or a steam jacket is wrapped round the base.

David Grant, of the old Speyside firm of William Grant & Sons, told me how they experimented recently with steam heating at Glenfiddich. 'We kept the product separate from the whisky we were making in the traditional coal-fired stills and we found that the steam firing changed the taste of the whisky. Adversely, in our opinion; it had less character. On the other hand at our other distillery, Balvenie, just a stone's throw away, we had experimented with steam heating and found it had no adverse effect. So Balvenie is steam heated and Glenfiddich isn't.' A distillery may replace its wooden washbacks with stainless steel ones and find that they've changed the taste of the whisky as well. Change for the sake of change when your customers are looking for consistency may come expensive.

The making of malt whisky is seen by Scottish distillers to be an art, whereas the making of beer or grain whisky is a science. Or as one whisky man put it: 'It's a stroke of good fortune that makes a malt distillery a good one; it's a stroke of engineering planning that can build a satisfactory brewery or grain distillery.'

There are other unmeasurable uncertainties which make it necessary for the Japanese to buy Scottish malts to top up their own indigenous 'whisky'. 'I've known a case,' I was told, 'where for one reason or another they dismantled a still and re-erected it in another corner of the same distillery — *it made a different spirit!*'

This didn't seem to me to be at all likely and I said so. 'Well, there could be a rational explanation. Perhaps, in the new place where they put it, the draughts were different and, therefore, the temperatures on the surface of the still were altered so that in the final analysis you collected more of one compound and less of another. It sounds strange but malt whisky is a strange thing — making it *is* an art. I often say that if a scientist went to Glenlivet he'd end up producing vodka.'

The Search for Consistency

In the early days, distilling was a seasonal occupation, undertaken during late autumn, winter and early spring when water was flowing plentifully in the burns. As soon as the barley was harvested, the making of whisky could begin; when all the grain had been used up and the water was no longer ice-cold, there was a 'Silent Season' between May and October. Now that most of the barley is malted mechanically the only reason a distillery has for closing is to give the staff their annual holiday. The 'Silent Season' has become just a holiday and annual maintenance break.

But there are experts who will tell you that they could, in certain circumstances, detect the difference between a January batch of whisky and a September batch. Ian Allen, manager of Bruichladdich, would go further: 'if you're at a distillery long enough you can get a very deep appreciation of your own whisky by nosing it every day. A man can nearly pick out what day of the week it's been produced. The Wednesday ester is different from the Thursday ester. Probably, if you had to state a preference, Tuesday would be the best because you're getting the first flush of the new wash through. On Monday you've been distilling what's been left over from the weekend. By the end of the week you're beginning to gather a few tails.'

Because a distillery is looking for consistency it will blend its week's production; but then a new problem appears. All whisky, whether it's malt or grain, has by law to be matured in cask for at least three years before it is sold, some malt whiskies are matured for much longer. Where the whisky is matured and what kind of cask it is put into can profoundly affect both the flavour and taste because every cask is different. 'If you fill a dozen casks in the same distillery on the same day,' a blender told me, 'and look at it twelve years later, all the samples will be different because of the effect of the cask.' People will tell you that these differences are quite fine. A whisky that's been matured for six summers and seven winters is discernibly different from a whisky that's been in cask seven summers and six winters. Whisky stowed near the roof of a warehouse will be different from the same distillation stowed on the floor.

So here is a spirit which is more complex, in many ways, than even Cognac. Gin can be made in the morning and drunk in the afternoon but malt whisky is a temperamental spirit which sometimes reaches its peak in five years but often takes three times that amount of time to mellow and reveal all its unpredictible secrets. Time then to find out how the minor miracle which transforms a foul-smelling yeasty porridge into an ardent elixir is accomplished.

What the Visitor Sees

A typical malt distillery will be pretty old. Fewer than twenty have been built in this century; the rest are nineteenth century, and a dozen or so were already in production in the eighteenth. For the industrial archaeologist, Scotland's distilleries present rich source material from the Age of Iron and Steam. But installed in the old buildings there may be shining new hardware which has reduced the workforce to a handful; whisky production is the least labour-intensive industry in Scotland. At Bruichladdich, for instance, the staff of ten can make up to 800,000 gallons of whisky a year.

The first thing that strikes one about a distillery is the comparatively few people around. None of the 43 distilleries owned by the giant Distillers Company have malting floors, so the men needed to tend the maltings are gone. Few distilleries have a full-scale cooperage for the making of casks any longer; perhaps a couple of men are employed on running repairs.

A surprising number of distilleries are still surrounded by wild country and there's no doubt that both geography and geology play an important part in the end product. It's probably true that the peat-covered hills in the Cairngorm drained by the Findhorn, the Deveron and the Spey rivers provide abundant supplies of the finest water. True, too, that the water from the Cromdale Hills in the middle Spey basin, flowing as it does over granite, influences the whisky more favourably than the water in the coastal areas round Elgin which has permeated through fluvio-glacial sands or old Red Sandstone.

The Barley

Wherever the distillery was sited, it formed part of the farming pattern, indeed was often an integral part of a farm. In the old days, the waste products of the distilling process — *draff* from the barley — would support a herd of cattle all through the winter; very often the barley itself was grown locally. It used to be said that the best barley came from the north-east, south of the Moray Firth and there are romantics who will claim that whisky hasn't tasted the same since the industry started using barley imported from England, Europe and Australia.

What the distiller is looking for is a grain that can be easily dried — so that it won't become mouldy when stored — rich in starch, not too high in nitrogen and protein and easy to germinate. First of all the barley is put through a dressing machine which removes any foreign bodies such as stones, animal

MALT WHISKY-POT STILL

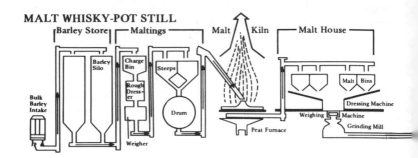

droppings, even pieces of metal. A strong magnet lifts these out of harm's way; a spark struck at the wrong moment could prove dangerous.

Malting the Barley

Then the barley is steeped in water until the moisture content is raised to just over 40 per cent. The vessels in which this is done hold about half a ton of barley and the period of immersion varies from 50 to 70 hours depending on the weather and the condition of the barley itself. It is then tested either with the fingers or, frequently these days, in the laboratory. When it is ready for germinating, the water is drained from the steep and the wet barley grains, if they are to be malted in the traditional way, are taken to the stone or concrete malting floor and spread with rakes to a depth of two or three feet so that the natural heat generated will trigger off germination.

When the barley has been raked out on the malting floor it is known as a *piece*; there may be up to half a dozen pieces being treated on the floor at any one time, all in different stages of growth. The process of changing the steeped barley into malt takes between nine and 12 days. As the piece lies on the floor it slowly begins to rise in temperature until it reaches 15°C. As soon as this happens, the barley is spread out, ankle high, to prevent it becoming overheated and turning into a spaghetti of tangled rootlets.

After eight to ten days on the floor, the barley will have sprouted and the growth is controlled by turning the piece with wooden shovels called *shiels* about three times every 24 hours. It is vital that the acrospire, the stem which would eventually grow through the soil from the planted barley, should not appear. If it does, the grain loses part of its value, so before this stage is reached the growth is halted.

In chemical terms the required amount of diastase and a small amount of maltose has been produced. The diastase enzyme renders the starch in the barley soluble and if you take a few

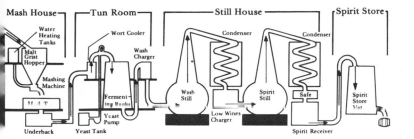

grains in your hand you'll find it soft and easily crushable. As an old maltman told Neil Gunn, 'When you can write your name on the wall with the ears it's ready.'

Peating the Malt

Now the *green malt*, as it's called, has to be dried in a *kiln* to kill the germ of the growing grain. In the old days malt was dried over peat fires — the only fuel available in many places. Today anthracite or coke is used but in the early stages peat is added to the fire and the pungent smoke is drawn through the wire screen on which the malt has been piled. The grains of green malt, still moist, are then virtually kippered in peat-reek and the aromatic compounds or phenols which they receive give malt whisky part of its characteristic flavour.

After peating, the kiln is heated to around 71°C until the malt becomes as crisp as toast. Malting by hand is a laborious process and nowadays most distilleries buy their already malted barley from centralised complexes. One of the largest in Scotland is Burghead maltings, on the Moray Firth between Findhorn and Lossiemouth. Built in 1966 at a cost of £1¼ million, it produces just under 70,000 tons of malt a year.

An advantage of the mechanical method of malting is that the process is temperature-controlled, so that malting can be done even in the heat of high summer. Large amounts of cool air are blown at controlled temperatures through the barley to regulate its growth and turning is only needed to prevent the rootlets from becoming tangled.

There are two common processes — Drum and Saladin malting. In Saladin malting the germinating barley is placed in long concrete boxes and conditioned air is blown by fan upwards through the grain. At Burghead, the grain is held in large metal drums which are rotated mechanically to turn the grain. In the Saladin system a paddle-type or screw-type turning machine moves along on top of the box and gently mixes the grain.

At Burghead, the drying kilns are fired by oil-burning furnaces

and the malt is peated in separate furnaces so that it can be given
the desired degree of peat-reek. The improved method of drying
and storing barley has progressively decreased the pre-war three
and a half months' silent season to a few weeks.

With a few picturesque exceptions, in most of the distilleries
you may visit, the first stage of whisky-making has been conducted
many miles away. The old malting floors no longer seethe silently
with the sprouting of the grain and that warm mouldy smell is
gone for ever. But that's the price of economic efficiency.

Mashing

The first process to be seen on a visit to a distillery may well be the
crushing of the malt in the mill-room to release the starch. By now
the malt has been 'dressed' to get rid of the tiny rootlets, known as
malt culms. Once it has been ground into a rough floury meal or
grist it is ready for mashing. It is mixed with hot water in the
mashing tun, a circular tank which may hold anything between a
thousand and five thousand gallons. At this stage the mash looks
like thin porridgy gruel. Now the Government in the form of the
resident Excise officer intervenes; from now on he will keep
precise and detailed records of the process. There is a strictly laid
down ratio between the amount of malted barley mashed and the
amount of spirit that can be expected to flow. Both the distiller
and the Excise Office do their calculations and if at the end of the
week the required gallonage of spirit is not forthcoming from the
mash the distiller may be liable to pay duty on the difference
unless he has a very good excuse.

While the water and the grist marry together, stirred and kept
at a critical temperature, the starch is converted into maltose and
dextrin and the sugary mixture that results is known as *wort*
(pronounced wurt). The liquor is drawn off and the residue is
mixed with more hot water, a process that is repeated until all the
sugar is removed. This process may last, depending on the
number of mashings made on the grist, for up to fifteen hours.
The solids left behind are processed, along with the malt culms,
and used for cattle food. The last mash (or last two mashes when
there are four), known as *sparge*, is added to the next batches of
grist to start the process once more.

Fermentation

The wort, when it is drained from the mash tun, is extremely hot
— between 70° and 82° C; so it is passed through a heat
exchanger which cools it to about 15° C before being gravity fed
or pumped to the *washbacks* — wooden or stainless steel vats
which can hold up to ten thousand gallons. Yeast is added to the
wort which immediately begins to ferment — there is much

boiling and foaming and a soapy scum rises to the surface. The commotion is caused by the enzymes of the yeast as they produce dextrose from the maltose in the wash and then convert it into alcohol and carbon dioxide. The wash is covered by a lid and if that is lifted for you to take a sniff then beware. The carbonic gas is highly concentrated and can hit you with the sharpness of an electric shock.

The fermentation continues for about 48 hours and the wash that results contains no more than ten per cent alcohol, it is not unlike a strong ale. Indeed the fermentation process is known as *brewing* and the distillery man who superintends it is called a brewer.

Every distillery has to provide full facilities for the Excisemen to check and measure the spirit at every subsequent stage of manufacture, maturing and bottling. It's rather like you or I having a permanent income tax official parked in the kitchen. What it means, apart from the vast amount of revenue collected, is that the Government is in effect an unwitting watchdog for the consumer as well. Since every gallon of spirit distilled is logged, it is almost impossible for a fraud to occur — nothing can be sold until it is three years old.

When fermentation has ceased, the fermented wort, known as the *wash*, is pumped to a *wash receiver* which in pre-war days used to be locked by the Excise officer. It couldn't be opened without his key and his approval but this is no longer considered necessary.

Distilling

The wash is now ready for the first distillation which occurs in pear-shaped *wash stills*. The stills, which are beaten out of copper, have gradually diminishing swan necks which lead to condensing coils or 'worms'. They rely on a simple scientific principle to extract the alcohol from the wash. In the first phase the wash is heated to a point above the boiling point of alcohol but below that of water. Inside the still, four rotating arms drag a copper chain mesh round the bottom of the still to prevent any insoluble matter from sticking there. This *rummager*, as it is termed, is not necessary when the stills are steam heated.

As the temperature of the wash rises, carefully controlled by the stillman who doesn't want it to boil over, the vapourised alcohol mounts into the neck of the still, runs over into the *condenser* and is there cooled, so that it resumes a liquid form. This liquid then flows into the *spirit safe* where the stillman can observe and measure it. This spirit safe sports a large lock and the Excise officer has the key. However, by the use of taps and handles placed outside the safe the stillman can not only control the destination of the running spirit but also measure its specific gravity. Inside the safe there is a glass jar with a hydrometer which can be filled with spirit drawn off for testing. Distilled water can also be introduced into the spirit samples to see what stage the distillation has reached. If the spirit turns cloudy when the water is added, the moment of truth has not yet come.

Making the Low Wines

The first vapours driven off and condensed are known as *low wines*. They are impure and not potable but the desired result has been achieved: the crude alcohol has been separated from the wash and the residue (*pot ale, burnt ale* or *spent wash* as it is variously known) is removed for processing into animal feedstuffs.

The object of the second distillation, in the *spirit still* is to extract the potable part of the distillate. The first flow, known as the *foreshots*, is strong and oily, containing as it does an excess of esters, aldehydes and acids — it is this unwanted spirit which when mixed with water turns cloudy. As the distillation continues the stillman keeps testing the foreshots until they give way to whisky. It is at this stage that he quickly moves the pipe in the spirit safe so that instead of flowing into the low wines receiver for redistillation the whisky, affectionately called the *middle cut,* is directed to the *spirit receiver.*

The whisky will continue to flow until it in turn begins to grow weaker. Testing it again and again with his hydrometer, the stillman eventually decides that the best has passed and the remnant of the distillation, known as *feints,* is channelled back to the low wines receiver or charger for redistillation. When the hydrometer indicates that water is beginning to flow this, known as *spent lees,* is run to waste. In these days of conservation and concern for ecology the spent lees are treated and cleaned before being discharged into any open stream or burn.

You'll notice in most distilleries that the wash stills are bigger than the spirit stills, because they have to deal with larger amounts of liquid.

Noticeable, too, in the still house are the different coloured pipes which run to and fro. Government decree requires that all pipes through which wash flows should be painted red; pipes through which low wines, feints or foreshots flow are painted blue; pipes through which clean spirit flows are painted black.

Cutting

Where the stillman 'cuts' his distillation — when, in other words, he decides the time has come to start collecting whisky — has a profound and irreversible effect on the finished product; no amount of mellowing and maturing can improve a whisky if it contains too many foreshots or feints. All distilleries have their own formulae for fractionating or dividing the distillation into its three parts — two unwanted, one precious. Generally speaking the whisky comes over at 25 to 26 over proof and while it is being collected it decreases in strength perhaps down to 5 over proof. Some distilleries cease collecting the spirit when it is eight over proof, others at five. If you cut low down you'll produce a heavier whisky because the heavier compounds will come over; if you cut high up, say at 12 over proof you'll produce a lighter whisky. If the process is hurried by heating the still intemperately a rough spirit will result, but if the stillman takes his time and lets his whisky trickle over gently from the condenser into the spirit safe he'll produce a full-bodied malt where the flavour elements have settled out. The ideal is to have no sudden surges, just a gentle flow from the still.

As Denis Nicol, the manager of Laphroaig, explained: 'We've got four stillmen and they're told "you'll cut at eight over proof" and that is it. But the point at which he goes from foreshots to middle cut, that is left for the stillman to decide. It might take an hour to clear foreshots, it might take ninety minutes, it's his judgment that is important.'

In Irish whiskey distilleries three distillations are common. The theory is that some of the undesirable higher alcohols will be more assiduously eliminated. Auchentoshan employs the triple distillation process, following a precedent which according to the Hebridean chronicler Martin Martin was practised in the Western Isles in the sixteenth century. There they distilled three times to produce a 'strong and hot' spirit known as *trestarig*. The ultimate potion was a four-times distilled spirit 'which at first taste affects all members of the body: two spoonfuls of this last liquor is a sufficient dose; and if any man exceed this, it would presently stop his breath, and endanger his life.'

The whole process from mashing the crushed malt to the collection of the whisky takes about a week. Before the last war no mashing or distilling was permitted in Scotland on the Sabbath and no distilling was permitted when mashing was going on. Today some of the bigger distilleries like Tomatin work a seven day round-the-clock week but a lot of them continue to enjoy a day of rest and some distilleries still devote one half of the week to mashing and the other to distilling, although it is now more general to carry out both processes side by side.

Maturing

When whisky comes from the still at a strength between 115° and 120° proof (Sikes), it will eventually be pumped from the spirit receiver to the *spirit store room* or vat — an operation once again done under the eagle eye of the Exciseman. The store has a double lock and needs two keys (Excise and distiller's) to open it.

Traditionally the spirit is now *reduced* (diluted is regarded as a pejorative word in distilling circles) by the addition of spring water to about 111°. The casks are checked and weighed in the presence of the Excise officer and the contents determined. As the whisky ages it will decline in alcoholic strength, perhaps, to 106° proof at around seven years and 100° proof after 12 years. At the time of removal to wood the spirit assumes an identity which will accompany it right up to the day of vatting or blending. Each cask is numbered and a very complete record of its contents is kept both by the distillery and the Exciseman in the bond book. From the spirit store room the whisky is moved to a bonded warehouse, equipped (in accordance with government specifications) with small, strongly barred windows and more double locks, where it will lie maturing.

Today the process of maturing is recognised as essential to produce a really good whisky; in the early days of smuggling, whisky was in such demand and its prolonged concealment so fraught with peril that nobody bothered to mature it. Even today many distillery workers prefer their whisky new and some resort to elaborate stratagems to sample the product at this stage, like lowering a tomato ketchup bottle through the bung of a barrel on a string. These primitive retrieval devices are known on Speyside as 'dogs'. In one famous distillery I was shown a small museum of dogs ranging from slim bottles to beautifully fashioned copper tubes for slipping down the trouser leg. Other trophies included inconspicuous body-shaped flasks which could be worn under the jacket to spirit the whisky past the gateman.

It's not only whisky that is smuggled out of distilleries. S. W. Sillett in *Illicit Scotch* (Beaver Books, 1965) tells of the Speyside worker who secreted wash in vacuum flasks and ran an illicit still in nearby Aberlour. Made in a couple of copper kettles, the spirit fetched £1 a bottle.

The Importance of Oak

By a law passed in World War One designed to conserve grain supplies it became illegal to sell any whisky until it had lain in cask for three years. The passing of the Immature Spirits (Restriction) Act in the Spring of 1915 may have inhibited a small section of the industry but for a long time the malt distillers had been aware of the value of ageing their whisky and many of them had found that malts needed not a mere three years in barrels but sometimes a slow development of up to 15 years.

In the days before bulk tankers were invented, all the sherry brought into Britain from Spain came in oak casks. When the casks were empty they went to Scotland to be refilled with new whisky. The Spanish wine-impregnated oak lent not only a darker colour to the clear spirit but also a variety of flavours. The other colour to the clear spirit but also a variety of flavours. The other day I was discussing the ageing of whisky with the head of a whisky house and he suggested that 'filling into sherry wood is the most inexact science that man has ever attempted. Whether it's Tio Pepe or Walnut Brown it's still classified as sherry wood but the difference in the final maturing can be marked.'

I remember a friend of mine, a distillery Exciseman, who kept on his sideboard two decanters. 'Fino', he would ask, 'or amontillado?' He drank his malt matured in a cask that had once contained amontillado; I preferred the fino.

Perhaps it was imagination that made us both detect a difference between the darker coloured whisky and the light. Certainly no distiller would want his whisky to taste of sherry. But as William Sanderson (of Vat 69 fame) wrote in 1864: 'It is well-known that Whisky stored in Sherry casks soon acquires a mellow softness which it does not get when put into new casks.' It is the softness that is prized, not the grapey overtones of Jerez.

Nowadays when it is becoming almost impossible to buy sherry casks in Britain, a certain proportion of malts are matured in wine-treated casks, others are matured in new casks, or casks which have already held whisky. These days, a great deal of whisky lies maturing in oak barrels that originally contained American bourbon. For reasons of health and safety, obviously discounted in this country, American law insists that Bourbon casks can only be used once, so they are broken down in the States, shipped to Scotland in *shooks*, and reassembled.

The decision to mature a malt in a particular kind of cask has an important effect upon its future development. The smaller the cask, the quicker the whisky matures. In a 110 gallon butt only 48 square inches of wood comes into contact with each gallon of whisky; in a 55-65 gallon hogshead the area is larger — 60 square inches of benign oak through which the spirit can evaporate its less desirable elements.

Both weather and situation play their part as well. As whisky ages it declines both in volume and strength. A whisky maturing in moist islands like Skye, Islay or Jura will lose its strength more quickly than its volume. Left to lie in a bone-dry warehouse, it will evaporate more quickly but retain more of its strength. All these variables have to be taken into account by the blender when he lays down his malts.

Nowadays many large firms remove their *fillings* as soon as they have been put in cask and mature them in their own warehouses. Wherever the casks are stored it is the custom to take weekly soundings to check that no accidental leakage is occurring. The Exciseman checks the casks now and again with a dipping rod and hydrometer to ensure that they are not leaking in other ways.

How Grain Whisky Is Made

Although in the late eighteenth century there was evidence that some distillers, in an ingenious effort to beat the licensing laws, were filling and emptying their stills up to a hundred times in 24 hours, the production of good whisky in a pot still was necessarily a slow process. In 1826 Robert Stein, a cousin of the Haigs and owner of Kilbagie distillery in Clackmannanshire, brought to completion a device for making grain whisky in a continuous process. John Haig erected a Stein Still at his Cameron Bridge works and paid a premium of a penny a gallon for the privilege to the Steins.

But it wasn't long before the Stein Still was superseded by a more efficient piece of machinery patented by Aeneas Coffey, a former inspector-general of Excise in Ireland. The Coffey or *patent still* as it became known also worked continuously and could use maize as well as barley. It had the further advantage of being so undemanding of peat and so economical with water that it could be sited conveniently in the centre of a town and not beside some remote Highland burn.

Today all Scotland's grain whisky distilleries, which between them produce about 2 million gallons of spirit a week, are situated in the urban Lowlands, close to ports and railway sidings — for they use prodigious quantities of grain. The two exceptions are the grain distillery at Invergordon, north of Inverness, which can turn out 30,000 gallons of spirit a day, and Ben Nevis, a former malt distillery near Fort William which in 1878 installed a patent still.

As an American once said lugubriously to me at Dover castle: 'Once you've seen one dungeon you've seen them all!' I'm afraid it's a remark which applies even more to grain distilleries. There are no aesthetically pleasing copper pot stills, no chances of seeing old men turning barley in a malting attic, just a highly efficient industrial process which can, as occasion demands, produce gin and vodka and all manner of industrial spirits.

Some Producers

The oldest grain distillery in Scotland is also the only one which offers its whisky in bottle. Cameron Bridge at Windygates, north of Buckhaven, installed a Stein Still in 1828 and a Coffey Still in 1832. *Choice Old Cameron Brig* is certainly a unique and historic grain whisky and I'm told that around Buckhaven some people drink it in preference to blended whisky. I have tasted it only once and found it pleasant and unexpectedly smooth.

Another equally old grain distillery, Cambus near Alloa, also marketed its grain whisky matured in wood for seven years and made some commercial play with the fact that it was a 'light, delicate, exquisite' whisky, compared presumably with pot still whisky which was heavy and indelicately polluted with congenerics. In their advertising the D.C.L. pictured a languid and patrician Edwardian connoisseur in white tie and tails, reclining in an armchair and raising his glass and affirming 'Not a headache in a gallon.' Cambus, ran the copy, was a 'soft, round, natural wholesome stimulant, that ministers to good health and neither affects the head nor the liver.'

David Macdonald of Macdonald & Muir, the Leith blenders who own Glenmorangie and Glen Moray, tells me that in the halcyon days when preposterous medical claims were part and parcel of the market place they put out a grain whisky which was announced as being specially suitable for diabetics. Macdonald & Muir's Diabetic Whisky has disappeared but grain remains, backbone of Scotland's biggest export industry.

When I visited the North British Distillery (one of two grain distilleries in Edinburgh) the Managing Director, Ian Fletcher, was at pains to impress on me that grain whisky is not a neutral spirit: 'A lot of people don't realise that it too has to be matured for three years.'

North British was set up in 1885 to counter the growing influence of The Distillers Company which had come into being in 1877. A group of whisky merchants and blenders under the leadership of William Sanderson opened their own distillery in 1885 'to be run and financed *by* the trade *for* the trade and thus to assure for blending purposes an independent supply of Grain Whisky of the finest quality at the most reasonable price consistent with sound finance.'

The firm, which is in many ways a co-operative of whisky blenders and merchants, holds no stocks of whisky on its own account and thus does not compete with its customers. The distillery was located close to the port of Leith and its supplies of grain, which come from as far afield as America and South Africa, reach the distillery by rail from the port and by road from other parts of the country.

In the sidings the railway vans specially constructed for

GRAIN WHISKY

carrying bulk wheat and maize are run over a hopper and the grain is dropped through chutes before being raised by elevators to the top of the granaries. The complex uses 20 tons of maize and seven tons of malt every two hours and the storage capacity is vast — when working to full capacity the distillery gets through 3000 tons of grain a month.

The barley is steeped and malted in Saladin boxes just as it would be for the pot still process and is then dried in oil-fired kilns. However, no peat is introduced at any stage. The bulk of the starch needed for the mash comes from maize which is ground into a fine consistency and cooked at high temperatures so that every particle can be exposed for conversion by the diastase of the malt into sugar.

The barley malt and maize are mixed with hot water, stirred for two hours until the starch has turned into sugar and then the contents of the mash tun are allowed to settle. The cereals fall to the bottom and the saccharine water or wort is pumped up to refrigerators, where it is cooled before being run to the fermenting vessels or wash-backs; yeast is added and fermentation takes place. The wash-backs, twenty of them, each hold 40,000 gallons, so one can appreciate the scale of the enterprise.

What the Visitor Sees

At the North British distillery they have two Coffey Stills each with a capacity of 8000 gallons an hour. Two towering columns rise through several floors of the building: the rectifier column consists of a continuous copper pipe (the relic of the ancient worm) which coils through a series of heavy wooden frames. Between each frame there is a perforated copper plate with a pipe leading to the frame below.

The wash is fed into the top of the rectifier column and it drops inside the copper pipe gradually to the bottom. From there it is taken to the second column (the analyser) and it flows by gravitation over steam to the bottom. As the steam rises, the wash travels back and forth over a series of perforated plates until it reaches the foot of the analyser. During its journey all the alcohols and more volatile liquids are vapourised and separated from the wash by the steam. The vapours are carried back into the bottom of the rectifier, passing inside the frames but outside the copper worm — these are known as feints vapours. They rise through the perforated copper plates inside the frames and, ingeniously, the vapours heat the wash descending *inside* the pipes while they themselves are cooled on the *outside* of the pipe.

The rising vapours consist of steam, ethyl alcohol (or whisky) and various higher alcohols. As each vapour condenses at a specific temperature it is possible, by carefully regulating the temperature at which the stills are working, to condense the whisky out at the desired moment. The rectifying process in the patent still removes many of the secondary constituents found in pot still whisky; consequently when it is reduced by the addition of water and put into casks it is altogether a milder product and requires less time to mature.

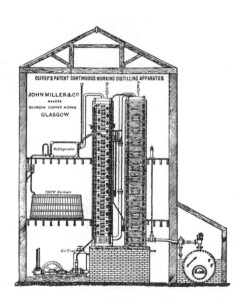

Contemporary diagram of a Coffey still

Malt Whisky Today

Had this book been written twenty years ago much of what follows would have been of only academic interest; single malt whiskies were then hard to come by outside Scotland. Indeed when Professor McDowall wrote *The Whiskies of Scotland* in 1967 fewer than 30 malts were available in bottle and he had to tell his readers that 'they have a limited appeal and are not generally sold.' Recently there has been a significant move in taste to the sampling and appreciation of malt whisky presented without the support, benign or dubious, of grain whisky.

In the nineteenth century malt whiskies were somewhat arbitrarily divided into five classes: Islay, Glenlivet, North Country, Campbeltown and Lowland. The accepted categories today are: Islay, Highland, Campbeltown and Lowland, although some would group Campbeltown and Islay together and describe them as West Highland.

The distinctions are not all that precise or all that useful. Talisker, produced on the Isle of Skye, is classed as a Highland malt and Isle of Jura is regarded by its owners as being more akin to a Spey malt than any other.

Highland Malts

These, the largest group of all, include the distilleries north of the Highland Line which roughly bisects Scotland from Greenock in the west to Dundee in the east. Further distinctions could easily and legitimately be made between the distilleries of Speyside, the ones to the north of Inverness and the island distilleries.

Historically the Highland malts were considered to be the finest of all, preferred in the early days of smuggling to the product of the licit Lowland distilleries which frequently used substandard wheat, unmalted grain and even oats and root crops in their mash. Folk memories die hard. In the summer of 1784 there was a dire shortage of bread in Edinburgh and a starving mob, convinced that the shortages were caused by distillers cornering supplies, attacked James Haig's distillery at Canonmills. Troops had to be called out and a rioter lost his life. The Haigs issued a statement claiming that 'not a grain of oats, pease or a particle of oat-meal, nor any potatoes, carrots, turnips or other roots are used in the distillery in any shape.' It was a canard put about, they claimed, by London distillers 'envious of the Scotch in the same trade (and) exerting their utmost influence to deprive the country of that valuable branch.'

The Highlands retained their reputation for good honest malt while the Lowland cities went on to become the great centres of grain distilling. Today there are 97 Highland distilleries ranging from Highland Park and Scapa on the Orkney mainland to Glenugie on the east coast and Glengoyne only half an hour's drive north of Glasgow. The oldest were built on sites of smugglers' bothies in the 1820s; the newest are Auchroisk and Pittyvaich-Glenlivet, which both went into production in 1974.

There is a tremendous variety here; some are full and heavy, others are light and subtle. To some you might apply the adjectives: delicate, fragrant, mellow, flowery and fruity. Others may seem rich, robust, pungent and peaty. Some are sweet, others sharp; some smooth, some hard. I don't really know whether it is possible to verbalise profitably about whisky any more than it is to spin evocative sentences about a *trockenbeerenauslese*. Some people derive pleasure from such preoccupations and there is no harm in that.

Lowland Malts

There are eleven malt distilleries south of the imaginary Highland Line; one of them, Bladnoch, enjoys the distinction of being the most southerly distillery in Scotland. Barnard, writing in the 1890s, was disparaging about them: 'Lowland malts alone, without Highland whiskies, would be of little use; the best makes are useful as padding when they have considerable age and not too much flavour, for they not only help to keep down the price of a blend, but are decidedly preferable to using a large quantity of grain spirit.'

Perhaps Lowland malts have suffered from their comparative closeness to the big industrial belt of Scotland; a distillery in an unspoilt mountain glen is more visually romantic than one set in the middle of a Clydeside town.

Among the Lowland malts Rosebank, owned by D.C.L., has always enjoyed a superior reputation and Auchentoshan, which employs a process of triple distillation, has its own distinctive quality. These two, along with Littlemill and Bladnoch, are the only Lowland malts available in bottle.

Campbeltown Malts

At one time there were 32 distilleries at work in the Mull of Kintyre with well-known names like Lochruan, Longrow, Rieclachan, Kinloch, Glengyle, Ardlussa and Benmore. Now only two remain — Glen Scotia, which dates from 1835 and Springbank (1828) which, like Auchentoshan, uses the triple distillation technique.

Campbeltown whiskies, dismissed by Barnard as 'generally thin, useful at the price' were then in great demand for blending. So great a demand that far too many of their proprietors cut corners to cash in on the whisky boom at the end of the nineteenth century. When demand for whisky slumped in the 1920s there was a move to the more consistent product of the Highlands. One by one the Campbeltown fires went out and the distilleries became bonded stores or were pulled down. One, Benmhor, has even become a bus depot. Only Springbank (at 80° proof and 12 years old) is available in bottle.

Islay Malts (pronounced *Eye*-ler)*

The eight distilleries on Islay — Ardbeg, Bowmore, Bruichladdich, Bunnahabainn, Caol Ila, Lagavulin, Laphroaig, and Port Ellen — provide an essential element in every blend. They have been disparaged as uncouth and unpleasant; they are certainly highly distinctive. Five of them are available as single malts and at a tasting of these five recently I was amazed at the subtle differences between them. The medicinal flavour of Laphroaig, the less powerful Lagavulin, the rich Bruichladdich, the fruity Bowmore and the peaty Ardbeg are all evidence that even in a micro-climate like Islay, the product of a pot still can be perpetually unpredictable.

How Malts Age

It is said that the Lowland malts mature more quickly than any others but again there is a high threshold of unpredictability. When marketing its whisky as a single, each malt distillery has to decide what is the optimum age. It will, of course, depend on the size of the cask, the character of the whisky, and the temperature and humidity of the warehouse.

There are few malt whiskies which improve beyond 15 years in cask. Recently I was taken into the warehouse at Glen Grant and offered a comparative tasting of 1959 and 1936. The older malt was no more than an interesting curiosity — at 42 years it had taken on unpleasant woodiness and was inferior by far to the

* see page 101 for other pronunciations.

19-year-old. David Grant of Glenfiddich tells me he prefers to drink his own product at eight years old rather than ten. So it's all very much a question of personal taste.

In 1977 for the Queen's Silver Jubilee a few distilleries were able to market a 25-year-old sample of their malt. Because whisky evaporates at the rate of around two per cent a year, keeping it for a long time not only ties up capital but results in a diminishing product. Glenfiddich's Jubilee Malt sold in Japan for £90 a bottle. 'The people who bought it,' David Grant told me, 'were pleased to satisfy their desire to have something that was special, rare, restricted and therefore highly sought after.' Very old blends, too, can command equally irrational prices.

Unlike wine, malt offers no outstanding years to remember, only outstanding malts, but it is possible occasionally to buy a malt whisky which declares the year of its distillation. As whisky is said not to mature in bottle it would be helpful if the year of bottling was also made a mandatory part of the labelling. A neighbour offered me a glass of 1962 Macallan's recently and we had an interesting few minutes trying to decide whether it was really 16 years old or whether it had perhaps been bottled in 1972 and was only ten years old.

Gordon & Macphail, Scotch whisky merchants of Elgin, who have the most varied and comprehensive list of malt whiskies in the world, are currently offering among their 53 listed malts the following 'vintages':

70° and 100° proof Talisker 1956/7
70° The Glenlivet 1938/9
70° Strathisla 1937/48
70° Macallan 1937/9

Many distilleries are resigned to seeing their malt bottled at 70° proof (the duty is lower and therefore the price more competitive) but the more distinguished the malt the more varied the combinations of age and strength. At the time of writing the following alternatives are available for these five malts all matured in sherry wood casks:

Whisky	Ages	Proof
Glenfarclas	8	70, 100, 105
	12, 15, 21	70
The Glenlivet	8	70, 80, 100
	12, 15	70
	15	80, 100
Glen Grant	8	70, 80, 100
	10, 15, 21, 25	70

It is also possible to buy 'clear' Glenfarclas and The Glenlivet, matured for eight years in white oak casks at 70° and 100° proof.

From this wide choice it is obvious that age, strength and the method of maturation are very much a question of individual taste.

Vatted Malts

The first 'blended' whiskies of all were the mixes made inside a distillery of that distillery's own malts — young mixed with old, winter malts mixed with spring, to acquire by 'vatting' a smoothing out of seasonal and age differences.

Vatting in the early days was a term strictly reserved to describe the blending of different casks of a single product. Today the term has been extended to cover the blending of various malts and there is a limited number of such old vatted malts on sale. Buchanan's market a blend of four 12-year-old malts they call Strathconon. It is, they claim, 'a Scotch whisky as it was drunk by connoisseurs a hundred years ago. There is no Scotch whisky quite like it available today . . . not peaty, pungent or smoky, but (with) a rich aroma, smooth flavour and a pleasing after-taste.' Findlater's have an eight-year-old vatted malt they call Mar Lodge: 'A whisky for the special occasion — to be savoured following a fine dinner, to be shared with friends of taste . . .'

Other vatted malts are Glen Drummond, Glen Eagle, Juleven, All Malt, The Seven Stills, Dewar's 12 years old, Capercailie, Glencoe, Hudson's Bay, Old Bannockburn, Royal Culross, Strathspey, Glenleven, and Duncraggan. There is, as far as I know, only one 'vintage' vatted malt and that is Pride of Strathspey, a blend of Speyside malts which were distilled in 1938/9. And there is only one vatted malt with a Hebridean provenance and that is the five-year-old Poit Dubh marketed by the Skye firm Praban na Linne. It was put on the market in 1978 as a good everyday malt for the local community. The company is one of several enterprises started by the pro-Gaelic Skye landowner, Iain Noble. 'Normally in the Highlands,' he told me, 'malts are drunk by visitors and tourists rather than by the Highlanders themselves, but we intend to keep the price of Poit Dubh as low as possible without economising on the quality of the whisky itself.'

At the time of the public enquiry which defined whisky in 1909 there were many people who felt that the malt distillers had lost their case by default — beaten at every turn by the superior purse and power of the grain distillers. Aeneas MacDonald described the verdict as 'Nothing short of a sin against the light to lump malt whisky with neutral industrial spirit as if it too were something to burn in lamps, to drive engines, or to clean clothes.'

If those are your feelings and you still want your whisky to be blended then a vatted malt may be the answer.

Blended Whisky

Was it a supply of blended whisky that created a demand for it, or a demand that promoted the supply? I can't tell you. On the one hand you could say that blended Scotch arose through commercial expediency; the whisky merchants realised that there could be a substantial economic advantage in mixing cheaper grain whisky with the more expensive and mercurial products of the pot still.

On the other hand you had whisky blenders like the Chairman of John Walker & Sons, who told a government enquiry that 'it is impossible to make whiskey in a pot still without getting much too great a flavour. You cannot reduce the flavour sufficiently to be sold *per se*. The grain whiskey, which can be made with a very small proportion of secondary products, may be admixed in order to bring down the flavour to a certain extent and keep it within popular taste.'

There was the argument, too, that whisky varied from bottle to bottle. Were you going to get a Glenlivet-type, an Islay, something from Campbeltown, a Lowland malt or even perhaps a bottle of grain whisky? All of those reasons led to the drink we know today as Scotch. In the 1860s, when blending grain and malt was in its early days, the production of patent and pot still whisky was fairly equal but by the end of the century, although the production of malt had soared to 14 million gallons, the grain distilleries were turning out 17 million gallons a year. Current production is running at 66 million gallons of malt whisky and 85.5 million gallons of grain a year.

The Business of Blending

Like all arts, blending is constantly changing. In the mid-1890s, the great Alfred Barnard compiled a little handbook on the art of blending for Mackie and Co., the precursors of White Horse Distillers Ltd. He warned against the use of 'prune wine, cheap sherries and other artificial maturing concoctions; they only make the whisky bilious and unwholesome, are the cause of a bad head and an ugly taste in the mouth in the morning.'

Barnard cited an example of a blend, two-thirds malt and one-third grain, that had achieved great popularity at home and abroad; in all probability it was White Horse itself as it was then composed:

3	Glenlivets	5 parts
2	Islays	3 parts
2	Lowland Malts	3 parts
1	Campbeltown	1 part
2	Grains	4 parts

Today these proportions are almost exactly reversed: the average blend is probably 70 per cent grain and 30 per cent malt.

In those competitive days, the ideal age of whisky in a blend was thought to vary with the consumer: 'for a high-class whisky for ordinary private trade the age should run from five to seven years, while for a public-house trade it should never be less than two and up to four years old. When blending it is always well to have a proportion, even if it be small, of very old for "top dressing" and giving an appearance of age; while it improves the bouquet it also adds to the average age of the blend.' Barnard reminded potential blenders that 'the first brands of Highland whisky are not procurable at a low price.' He preached the virtues of laying aside a blend for six months or so in cask in order to let its constituent parts marry.

All sound advice, and yet perhaps to our taste those turn of the century blends would seem heavy and unpalatable. One of the best noses in the business, Charles Craig of Invergordon Distillers, told me that he had once got hold of a case of pre-1914 whiskies; as he recalled them, his sensitive nostrils wrinkled: 'Those whiskies were very very inferior, I can't stress it too strongly. Rough, coarse, big, ugly — a grain and a couple of malts slung together.'

What makes for perfection in today's blends? Everyone is agreed that if you haven't got the right whiskies at your disposal then you're going to make pretty discordant music. As one blender said: 'Today we're using between 30 and 40 whiskies in a blend as opposed to ten or so pre-war. It *is* like an orchestra. The individual players may be brilliant, so are the best malts, but someone has to make the individual players harmonise and a top blender has the same function as a first rate conductor. He uses Speyside to give it this lovely phenol character, Islay to give it strength, Lowland to give it volume, grain to give it background and not kill the thing with fusel oil and so on.'

With duty in Britain at well over £3 a bottle the difference between a good blend and a bad blend in terms of cost is not all that significant today. The main problem is the availability of the whiskies.

This is one of the reasons for the emergence of a huge company like D.C.L., with its 43 malt distilleries and its vast output of grain whisky — resources which provide both variety and long term continuity for its blenders. In the early days of the whisky industry a blender might well have to rely on what he could pick up in the market place and frequently, in the interests of economy, he would succumb to the temptation of buying as cheaply as possible. Today the big blending houses plan their production years in advance.

So in 1980 casks will be sent for filling to distilleries all over Scotland and some of their contents will not finally flow together until the turn of the century. The price of fillings varies remarkably little between one distillery and another. The opening prices in January 1978, for instance, for grain whisky, due to an international fall in the price of maize, were lower than in 1977. Whereas in 1977 they were all quoted at 93p a proof gallon, the 1978 prices varied from 89p for Port Dundas and Carsebridge to 92p for the rest.

Malt prices were kept in 1978 at the same level as in 1977, ranging from 200p per proof gallon to 213p. If you are tempted by the thought of making a gallon of your own whisky for £2 there is nothing to stop you. All you have to do is apply for a licence — the annual cost is roughly the price of three bottles of Scotch. But there are a few snags. Your premises would have to be of commerical size and they would have to be approved by the Excise people before you could begin distilling. You couldn't, in other words, do it in the garden shed. And of course you wouldn't be able to invite your friends round to sample it for at least three years.

To return to reality. If a blender wants a 12 year old Glenlivet, or an eight year old Lowland, then someone twelve and eight years previously must have laid down that whisky in anticipation. These days that 'someone' is usually the blending house itself, frequently owning its distilleries and therefore in a position to exchange fillings with other companies.

Invergordon Distillers, for instance, own Tamnavulin, Ben Wyvis, Deanston, Tullibardine and Bruichladdich and the Invergordon grain distillery with a combined output of 13 million gallons a year. Although they are one of the largest independent whisky companies in Scotland, their own distilleries do not provide them with the variety of malts which they need for their blends. So they swap: 'We send out casks for filling to other distilleries whose malt we need; they send their casks to Bruichladdich or Tamnavulin. This is how we have available 70 or 80 malts when we only own five.'

In this way whisky can be laid down without any money changing hands. Although some whiskies are more expensive when matured than others, the cash differences per gallon between them as new spirit can be measured in pennies. 'With most other malt distilleries,' one distillery owner told me, 'we exchange barrels on a one to one basis. We'll fill a barrel of his in return for him filling a barrel of ours. With grain, that's slightly different; for five barrels of our malt we'd get nine of grain. There are so few of us left as independents that we all know each other. We just pick up the 'phone and settle it like that.'

The Secret Formulae

Blenders are highly secretive about their formulae. I asked five companies if they would divulge the contents of their blends and they all declined. Few would specifically tell me what proportion of their whisky was grain, what malt. A notable exception was Adam Bergius, chairman of Teacher's and also chairman of the Information and Development Committee of the Scotch Whisky Association. It used to be part of the industry's philosophy to claim that there was no such thing as bad whisky. Mr. Bergius does not go along with that specious line of thinking: 'We did ourselves great harm talking like that. I think there's an enormous difference between one blend and another. If the public were as devoted to appraising blends of whisky as they are to discussing wine and beer we would have a much healthier market.'

Perhaps that hasn't been entirely the fault of the public. It's only in the last 15 or 20 years that distilleries have opened their doors to visitors. Some are still unable to believe that showing potential customers around might be in the long run beneficial. There is a traditional secretiveness about what goes in the bottle, although many people in the industry believe this to be counter-productive, among them Mr. Bergius: 'I think we should be more specific and tell people what proportion of malt and grain we put in. We're very happy at Teacher's to do it, our blend is very close to fifty-fifty and the principal malts are Ardmore and Glendronach. Everyone knows Teacher's must contain Ardmore because we don't sell Ardmore to anyone else and we don't sell it as a malt, so unless we're pouring it down the drain it must go into the blend.'

So that's one way, indeed the only way, of finding out what the principal constituents of a blend might be. A company owning distilleries must be happy with its product and will use a large percentage of the output in its own blends. Indeed securing the ownership or at least a significant interest in good malt distilleries has always been the prime strategy of the ambitious blender.

But not everyone in the industry would agree that revealing the proportion of malt whisky and grain whisky in a blend would be all that helpful. As one blender told me: 'There are malts which I would say are not good; they are just ordinary and have no distinction whatsoever. You see single malts on sale in supermarkets that you wouldn't put into a blend, much less sell as a single. There are at least 20 distilleries I wouldn't give the very smallest house room to and another 15 where you'd have to give me a very good reason to take even a small filling.'

It is the selection of the malts, followed by their judicious blending with the right kind of grain whisky, that makes a really good blend and although the proportion of grain to malt is important it is perhaps not the most important factor. Another blender put it this way: 'There are whiskies going out of Britain in bulk for sale in German supermarkets which are near enough 95 per cent grain and 5 per cent malt. That balance is all wrong and probably the blend has just been slung together by some fly-by-night firm. But it's not true that the higher the proportion of malt the better the blend. You can have a really superb collection of well-matured, intelligently chosen malts mixed with first class grain whisky, say in the order of 35 per cent malt and 65 per cent grain, and you get a first class blend. On the other hand you may have a whisky with 65 per cent malt and 35 per cent grain but if the malts are poor ones, badly chosen, perhaps matured in the wrong cask, inadequately warehoused, of the wrong age . . . then you've got an inferior blend.'

The idea of the perfect blend probably only exists in the perfect blender's mind but the final product still is, as it was in Barnard's day, something 'so perfect that it strikes the consumer as being one liquid, not many — i.e. having absolute unity, tasting as a whole.'

Getting it all together

Once a formula has been produced that takes the public's fancy, then a blender sticks scrupulously to his success. 'If you've got it right,' a blender said, 'you stay there; in fact you become almost paranoiac about staying there.'

I talked to a blender who was responsible for the mixing of 1800 casks a week. Each one is 'nosed' in case there should be some defect. It may be a rusty nail in the barrel or a mustiness, a stale smell the experienced blender detects instantly: 'Maybe seven or eight times a year you'll get a barrel which smells stale. It has a deadening effect on the whisky. Instead of a full lively round whisky it has a coppery, metallic taste. We'll send the sample to the laboratory and they'll give us a safe dilution for it but what really happens is that we stick it in a corner and pretend it isn't there. It's not catastrophic in money terms — we're talking about £50 or so — but it's the trouble it causes. If we lost one cask of grain in a blend it wouldn't matter too much but if you lose a malt then you have to get something to replace it so that you don't upset the balance of the whole blend. We have a buffer stock of single barrels in the warehouse just in case a bad barrel does turn up.'

Many blends contain up to 35 different malts and with that number juggling is possible. 'If a distillery catches fire or has to close down for three months to do a major repair then you may find at some later stage you're short of A or B which has always been a component of the blend. But a skilful blender will have something else on hand, a little bit of C or D which has a similar character. But if five of your major components disappear overnight, then no way can you keep your blend the same.'

The Role of the Cask

The casks of whisky themselves may have been maturing in a firm's central bonded warehouse, or they may have been left in the distillery of their origin. Each distillery will have barrels maturing on its own premises. Some will be reserved for the parent company's blends or for bottling as a single malt; the rest may be awaiting ultimate collection from the owner.

At Bruichladdich on Islay the manager, Ian Allen, explained how each cask has its own computerised identity: 'Because the wood plays such an important part in the maturing, you must know which is which. If a blender sends for cask 4053 of 1977 he knows from his records that when filled it was 112.1 gallons; he knows the strength because when we fill it we send him a copy of the details. So if they want it sent to Elgin for blending, off it goes.' A cask ageing at Bruichladdich might over a period of 14 years lose 15 per cent of its volume. The Excise, generous for once, allow a distillery to write off 2 per cent overall a year, so there are small gains to be made depending on temperature and humidity.

One of the largest warehouses in Scotland is the vast complex near Stirling owned by Scottish Grain Distillers, yet another D.C.L. subsidiary. There are 49 individual warehouses, each twice as long as a football field, lying in the shadow of the Ochil Hills. The hogsheads are stacked ten high in vast and silent hangars. The value of the whisky is £290 million. If on some mad whim D.C.L. wished to take it all out of bond at once they would have to hand over around £4,030 million pounds to the Exchequer!

Every day the equivalent of 33,000 bottles evaporates; every working day another 1000 casks of new malt whisky arrive and 2000 of grain. They stay for periods of between three and twelve years, lying in a temperature of between 10° and 13° C until they are called in for blending. Although there was a cutback in production in 1974 when D.C.L. reduced its distilling programme by 14 per cent, it was announced in June 1978 that they were to go ahead with plans for 34 new warehouses able to hold about 45 million gallons on a 260-acre site in Stirlingshire.

The actual operation of blending the whiskies is comparatively simple. The chosen barrels are emptied one by one into a stainless steel blending trough and run into vats where they are mixed either mechanically or nowadays mostly by the action of compressed air. The blend is then stored in oak casks or stainless steel vats for another six months before bottling.

Some firms blend their grains and malts before the final maturing, others blend them at the time of bottling. Before bottling, the blend is reduced to 70° proof for the British market or whatever strength is required for export. It is cooled to 7°C and filtered through diatomite after reducing to eliminate any insolubles which might possibly make the blend cloudy.

It is customary to colour whisky with caramel to produce a consistent appearance from batch to batch. In the last few decades fashion has moved to straw-coloured whiskies and away from the sherry colour favoured formerly. As most people seem to associate depth of colour with strength this might seem to indicate that, psychologically, whisky drinkers wish to appear to be drinking more circumspectly than before. Light coloured Scotch became popular in America long before it did in Britain.

Pedigree on the Label

A word might not be out of place here about the descriptions that can be legally applied to whisky. The terms: *de luxe, old, very old, rare old, old matured, V.V.O., special, extra special, supreme, real, private stock, private cellar, three star, antique, liqueur, fine & rare, finest* have only the connotations which the chap who writes the label wishes to put on them. What to one firm may be very old and rare and precious may be to a competitor anything but. Blenders are notoriously chauvinistic about their own brands and who can blame them? If you don't have infinite faith in the product how can you sell it?

The Brand to Choose

Although there are over two thousand brands of blended Scotch produced for sale on the home market and even more for export, (most of them blended and bottled in Glasgow, Edinburgh, Perth, Montrose, Elgin and Kilmarnock), the bulk sales are in the hands of a very few firms. In 1977 just under 70 per cent of the market was held by ten brands:

Bell's	16 %
Teacher's	12¼ %
Haig	10 %
Grant's	6 %
Johnnie Walker	5 %
White Horse	5 %
The Famous Grouse	4 %
Dewar's	4 %
Whyte & Mackay	3½ %
Vat 69	3½ %

The Role of the Broker

Although the big firms review their stocks on a six-monthly basis and project their potential demands far ahead into the future, there are occasions when a sudden upsurge in sales may place them at a temporary disadvantage and it is then, if telephoning around doesn't produce the whiskies wanted, that they might seek the services of a broker.

The broker's function is to balance any deficiencies in stock which a big blender may meet. Before World War Two they used to reckon on a 5 per cent gap between what a company might require and what it would lay down; nowadays (computers perhaps?) the gap is more likely to be 2 per cent — so the modern broker is in a declining industry, playing a small role in the marriage market of grains and malts.

The bigger brokers will fill casks of whisky on their own account in the hope that such speculative enterprise pays off over the years. And it often does. In addition to the large companies with international names there are smaller companies on the fringe of the market who, lacking the finance for long-term investment, buy their whisky on the open market after it's been matured.

Some of these firms lend distinction to the industry; others do not. For them it is a quick operation; they buy their whisky, bottle it and get paid in a few weeks.

Other firms may have a potential outlet in a supermarket chain in Europe. One reputable broker told me: 'There's a lot of rubbish leaving the country. One blend is being shipped out to Europe at the moment in bulk at about £1.40 a gallon — that's 17p a bottle. Even including bottling, labelling, handling and everything that's well below the Scotch Whisky Association's miminum recommended price of £11.15 a case.'

Twelve years ago whisky looked like being a good investment and there was a lot of it made, but as in other forward planning there is a strong element of risk. The cost of making a gallon of whisky in 1974 was £1.40; in 1978 it was selling for about £2. If the market suddenly got stronger it could rise to £4 but as a broker knows, if he fills whisky today at £2 a gallon there is no guarantee that he will be able to place it at a profit in four years' time. If the big companies have a surplus and flood the market then the price could slump disastrously. There are speculators who are caught with too much whisky; to recoup their losses, as a whisky executive put it, 'they stick it all together and call it a blend and make some deal somewhere.'

Scotch in Export Markets

In a supermarket in Evian in the summer of 1978, alongside White Horse, Black & White and Vat 69, I saw a bottle of reduced size which bore the following label:

Fin Whisky

HAMPTON

Blended Whisky
ce whisky est composé de pur malt
importé d'Ecosse et d'alcool de grain
Français

At Frs 23.50 it must have seemed a bargain to the uninformed — the veritable whiskies from Scotland were ten francs more. Alongside it was another whisky I had never heard off. This proclaimed itself (again at Frs 23.50) to be *De Luxe,* thus putting itself somewhat impertinently in the same class as Chivas Regal (Frs 80).

'Scotch Whisky. Aged 3 Years,' the label read, 'SALISBURY. De Luxe. Aged and Blended in Scotland.' A blend containing 3 year old whiskies and posturing as *de luxe* is the kind of sharp practice that does the industry more harm than good.

The German firm of Racke has solved the problem of mixing unrevealed quantities of Scottish malt whisky with home-produced alcohol and giving it market appeal by inventing the almost untranslatable word *rauchzart: Rauch* is smoke and *zart* is tender, but through steady use of the phrase in advertising campaigns 'smoke-tender' has begun to acquire an image almost as valuable as peat itself — perhaps more valuable. 'It needs more than a peat fire to make a Whisky *rauchzart,'* ran a recent full page advertisement in *Der Spiegel.* What it needs apart from old malt whiskies bought for *viel gutes Geld* are 'Germany's tender grains' made from the 'famous wheat that grows in the Hildesheim plains' and the skill of Herr Georg Habermann, 'the only *Whisky-Blend meister* in Germany.' And sales boom. Well may Racke cry *Zum Wohl!*

It is not Germany nor France that is seen as the real threat to Scotch whisky but Japan, which for a long time now has been importing malt in bulk to lend a Scotch taste to its own whisky. Up to a third of a bottle of the up-market Japanese whiskies like Suntory may be Scottish malts. In 1977 six million gallons of malt whisky were shipped to Japan, provided principally by Tomatin Distillers (Tomatin is the most productive malt distillery in Scotland), Hiram Walker (owners of Glenburgie, Milton Duff, Pulteney, Balblair, Scapa and Glencadam) and The Glenlivet Distillers (Benriach-Glenlivet, Caperdonich, Glen Grant-Glenlivet, The Glenlivet and Longmorn-Glenlivet) in which Suntory had a 12 per cent holding. With the successful takeover of Glenlivet Distillers by Seagrams in 1978 this lucrative and expanding bulk malt export market is now dominated by Canadian-based firms.

As well as buying themselves bargaining power in Scottish malt distilleries, the Japanese are busy building their own and they are believed to have an annual production of 11 million gallons. David Grant of Glenfiddich, the malt whisky which has captured a third of the international market, personally deprecates the export of bulk malt whisky to Japan: 'I believe that Suntory does pose a serious threat to Scotch whisky in overseas markets. Any firm which is operating off a home base of 20 million cartons a year — that's larger than the whole UK market put together — can easily afford to establish itself in other countries — the U.S. for instance, or Australia, by price-cutting. I am totally opposed to helping them improve the quality of their product at our expense.'

In 1975 eight million gallons of bulk malt left Scotland for Japan, Brazil and Argentina to improve lesser whiskies. The trade unions in Scotland are opposed to the export of whisky unbottled because, they say, it's costing 6000 jobs a year. In terms of malt exports, firms which are selling bulk malt overseas may be doing Scotland an eventual disservice. Perhaps they should all be taken by bus to Evian and forced to drink a bottle of *Fin Whisky Hampton*.

Value for Money

As with any product which suffers from a high Excise duty based not on quality but quantity, the more you pay for a bottle of Scotch the more value you are getting in terms of the contents. This may mean not only a higher proportion of malt whisky compared with grain but also a higher proportion of malts chosen more for their excellence and their blending potential than their price. Since the art of blending is to take each individual malt at the peak of its maturity the difficulty of producing a really outstanding blend is completely negated by having to work to a budget.

Once they are blended, whiskies, like a shinty team, do not necessarily all age smoothly together. One firm which marketed an eight year old blend for the American market matured it for a further four years and then decided to sell it in Britain as a 12 year old blend. But they found that the extra four years in cask had worked against the blend, not in its favour.

Age can be deceptive. Perhaps impressed by Old Cognac, old port and indeed old clarets, many people with more money than knowledge demand blends of whisky which are far older than they need be. You can, if you wish to pay the premium price, buy blends lavishly packaged in beautifully sculpted decanters, which are 15 or more years old, but you are often paying for their *réclame* not their excellence. As one blender put it: 'A 15 year old blend is a nonsense and anything older than that is a sheer waste of time and money. That there should be 15 year old whiskies in a blend is quite acceptable and indisputable but to put every whisky in a blend at 15 years old is folly. No grain whisky improves after, at the very outside, eight years so who are you kidding?'

In the final analysis it is not age alone that matters but, as one whisky enthusiast put it, a dedication to a certain degree of extravagance: 'Nowadays you have guys in white coats called chemists who are supposed to be improving things but at the end of the day they are there to get more not less from a bushel of malt. But you don't want more, you want the best. When you're distilling you must not be under an obligation to expand the bit in the middle by taking too much of the foreshots. It takes integrity to waste the product. Whether its a Rolls Royce or a good suit or a good dish there's a certain amount of extravagance required. I'm a great believer in extravagance!'

For those who want that little bit extra in a blend I have listed in Appendix 2 some of the blends which have been put together with some extravagance; space forbids all.

A still house at Nevis distillery, Fort William

7

The Names on the Labels

There are several reasons for the gradual emergence of blended whisky drinking, not least the aggressive and often inspired marketing of their product by the great Scottish blenders and merchants of the nineteenth century.

The preferred spirit among the English upper classes in early Victorian times was brandy and seltzer or soda. When they weren't tippling brandy, they were consuming prodigious quantities of champagne, claret, burgundy and port. But when the sap-sucking aphid *phylloxera vastatrix* made its first appearance in the south of France in 1863, probably imported from America in a cargo of fruit, the Scots got their big chance. As the French vineyards fell to the ravages of the invader and cognac and wine soared in price the English discovered the consolations of whisky, which they found not all that inferior to brandy and appreciably cheaper.* In 1896 The Victoria Wine Company, London's biggest chain of off-licences, was selling eight year old brandy ('the acme of perfection') at 7s 1d a bottle, whereas you could have a ten-year-old blend of finest Scotch whisky for only 3s 10d.

Anyway the opportunity was seized and Scotch began its long ascendancy both at home and abroad as the world's favourite and universal spirit.† Considerable fortunes were amassed, peerages were conferred, dynasties founded and family names made

* And perhaps few people noticed any difference between brandy and whisky when diluted with soda water, unless palates were more perceptive than they are today. At a blind tasting arranged for whisky distillers, cognac shippers, and wine writers by the British magazine *Decanter* in 1977, fewer than a third of the experts were able to distinguish between cognac and malt whisky, let alone pass judgement on their respective merits.

† So universal that it is the only beverage to find a place in the International Phonetic Alphabet used in the world of aviation '. . . Victor, *Whisky,* X-ray, Zebra.'

familiar in saloon bars all over the country — Haig, Dewar, Buchanan, Walker, Bell and Teacher. They represent an alphabet of great interest for the student of social history and the drinker curious to know more about the name on the bottle.

Bell's

Arthur Bell was perhaps typical of the early blenders. In the 1840s he joined a Perth wine, spirit and tea firm as a travelling salesman. By 1851 he was a partner and responsible for whisky sales. In those early days their blend had only one Highland malt in it, Edradour; the remainder, malt and grain, came from the cheaper Lowland distilleries. But when he took the firm over in 1865 he was already experimenting more ambitiously. He was well aware that 'several fine whiskies blended together please the palates of a greater number of people than one whisky unmixed, consequently I have long adopted that practice, and never found it necessary to send out showcards but just allowed the qualities of my goods to *speak for themselves*.' Much of his blends were sold in cask and he used neither trade mark nor label, but his sons saw the advantages of brand names and today the name of Bell on a bottle, although there hasn't been a Bell on the board since 1942, is one of the most respected in the trade.

Black and White

Another name that survives to the present day is that of **James Buchanan**, whose career illustrates the vast profits that an ambitious entrepreneur was able to make in the buccaneering heyday of unfettered private enterprise. Born in Canada of Scottish immigrant parents, he was brought back to Scotland, schooled in Ireland and at the age of 14 began work as an office-boy in a shipping agent's at four shillings a week. When he died in 1935 his estate was valued at £7 million.

At 19 James joined his brother, who was a grain merchant; later he was appointed London agent of a Leith whisky firm. Offered some capital in 1884, he set up in business on his own account. What he set his mind on 'was to find a blend sufficiently light and old to please the palate of the user. This I fortunately was able to do, and I made rapid headway.' By the time of Queen Victoria's jubilee in 1887, the Buchanan Blend was to be found in every bar and the whisky boom was just about to begin. A born salesman, James pushed his blend at home and overseas and revealed a flair for showmanship. His interest in racing and horses extended to commerce as well as pleasure. Every morning at his Holborn premises whisky was loaded for distribution round London. 'The vans,' recorded *The Times*, 'were uniformly smart with paintwork that was glass-like in its finish. The coachmen and trouncers, with their silvery-grey toppers, were clad in blue uniforms modelled on that worn by James Selby who took the "Old Times" coach from London to Brighton and back in seven hours, 50 minutes in 1888.' It wasn't until May 1936 that the firm, to universal grief, gave up their horse-drawn vehicles.

One of Buchanan's best known blends was put up in a black bottle with a white label and known as 'House of Commons.' The public began to ask for 'the black and white whisky' and it was Buchanan himself who suggested the black and white terriers which are still a part of the success of Black & White. He twice won the Derby, and was certainly the most famous whisky promoter of his day. In 1978, Buchanan & Co. (since 1925 a part of D.C.L.) announced the re-introduction of the brand name *The Buchanan Blend* which had been used in the nineteenth century for the whisky supplied to members of the House of Commons.

There is a pleasing story told of Buchanan's suspicion of Lloyd George, who was selling peerages to the wealthy in return for contributions to Liberal party funds. It was Lloyd George, a crusading anti-drink Prime Minister, who was responsible for increasing the tax on whisky by a third in his 1909/10 budget — obviously a man to be approached by a Scot with considerable caution. Buchanan, who was by then a baronet, was offered a peerage; being canny he chose a title and signed the cheque 'Woolavington' thus ensuring that it couldn't be cashed until he had indeed been publicly confirmed as the new Lord Woolavington.

Dewar's

Although James Buchanan had promoted his blends with flair and fervour, he was by no means the first merchant to realise that the English palate required something lighter than the heavy Highland malts. The English had originally encountered whisky on the banks of salmon rivers, on grouse moors and deer forests and in the antlered interiors of icy Highland shooting boxes. After a hard day's slaughtering, a few strong malts worked wonders, but back in London something less substantial was needed.

Thomas Dewar, who set up as a wine and spirit merchant in Perth in 1846, was the first to put his blends in a bottle. His sons, John and Thomas, encompassed the world with their whisky; they acquired their own distilleries and their baronies — John who remained in Scotland became Baron Forteviot of Dupplin and his younger brother 'Whisky Tom', who like James Buchanan had taken to horse-racing and the Home Counties, became Baron Dewar of Homestall, Sussex. Whisky Tom was a great crony of Sir Thomas Lipton the grocer, and was frequently in the company of the Prince of Wales, later King Edward VII, who was stimulated by wealth and success in every form. It was said that the Prince had the first car in England, Tea Tom Lipton the second and Whisky Tom the third. Both Whisky Tom and James Buchanan traded on their Scottishness. Tommy Dewar's first move on coming to London at the age of 21 was to bring a piper in full tartan to the Brewers' Exhibition at the Agricultural Hall in Islington, where he had rented a stand. The staid English brewers, who had never been exposed to whisky merchants at their annual jamboree, let alone the skirl of bagpipes, were outraged. But Dewar came back the following year and on the stand next door was his great rival Buchanan.

A frequent visitor to Dewar's Sussex estate was that walking symbol of music hall Scotland, Sir Harry Lauder. If Glasgow belonged to Harry Lauder, Tommy Dewar had already made his blazing mark on London by setting up a huge electric moving sign on the old shot tower by Waterloo Bridge. It depicted a bearded and be-sporraned Highlander jerkily knocking back dram after dram of White Label from an apparently bottomless bottle. It was perhaps the way all the whisky barons liked to think the product could be imbibed — endless consumption with no visible ill effects.

In case you have gained the impression that the early whisky salesmen were locked in ruthless and singleminded battle with each other, it is only fair to point out that Tommy Dewar went on record with the thought that 'competition is the life of trade, but the death of profit.' It was no surprise when he and James Buchanan merged their companies in 1915.

White Horse

Six years younger than James Buchanan and nine years older than Whisky Tom was another seminal figure in the story of blended Scotch. His nickname was 'Restless Peter' and he looked in later life not unlike a Hollywood actor playing an eccentric English peer, although unlike his other two contemporaries **Sir Peter Mackie** never achieved a barony. Perhaps it was his relentless Tory opposition to Lloyd George, who drew a great deal of his electoral support from the nonconformist Temperance vote, that put paid to that. Lloyd George's infamous whisky-bashing budget, Mackie declared, was the work of a 'faddist and crank, not a statesman. But what can one expect of a Welsh country solicitor being placed, without any commercial training, as Chancellor of the Exchequer in a large country like this?'

Sir Peter Mackie in monocle and Highland evening dress was a daunting host. If you were unlucky you might easily find yourself being indoctrinated with his latest restless enthusiasm: tweed-making, the prefabrication of concrete blocks, carragheen moss or the manufacture and distribution of a special flour by which he set great store. It was called BBM, the initials standing for Brain,

Bone and Muscle. He insisted that all his employees should use BBM in their homes.

A powerful opponent of the use of young raw whisky in blends, he campaigned unsuccessfully for a fiscal system which would impose a diminishing tax on whisky based on its age. 'Young cheap, fiery whisky' which he claimed was 'responsible for most of the riotous and obstreperous behaviour of drunks' should attract the highest rate of tax, old mature whiskies the lowest. Although he lost that battle he, more than any man, was responsible for the success of White Horse whisky, a blend which originally contained Lagavulin, Craigellachie, and grain whisky.

Peter's uncle, James Logan Mackie, pioneered the blend in the 1880s and it has become one of the most successful in the world — so well known in fact that on Restless Peter's death in 1924 the firm changed its name to White Horse Distillers. A man of fierce independence, Peter had resisted all the blandishments of D.C.L. and it was not until three years after his death that White Horse became part of that huge and disparate consortium.

Haig

Older by far than the Buchanans, the Dewars, the Mackies and the Bells was the ancient Norman family of Haig who established themselves in the Lowlands of Scotland early in the 12th century. By the 17th century they were distilling *uisge beatha* and it was a **John Haig** who founded the original grain distillery at Cameronbridge, based on the continuous still designed by his cousin Robert Stein. A later John Haig became a founder member of the Distillers Company when it was formed in 1877 but perhaps the most famous member of the family was Field Marshal Sir Douglas Haig, a director not only of Cameron Bridge distillery but also of the appalling carnage of Passchendaele.

An early advertising motto of the Haigs was 'D'ye ken John Haig?' which was later replaced by the even more internationally known slogan: 'Don't be vague, ask for Haig.' That and their famous 'Dimple' bottle gave them an unchallenged place in the whisky market and in the inter-war period they sold more Scotch than any other firm in Britain.

By the outbreak of World War Two, the United States had become Scotland's biggest customer and it was a cargo of whisky, including the highly-prized Haig, on its way to earn valuable dollars, that went aground in the Hebrides on a February night in 1941. By a perverse but benevolent piece of mis-navigation the S.S. *Politician* stuck fast in the shallow Sound of Eriskay. There were six casks of whisky on board and 243,600 bottles and when the crew had departed the islanders descended on the stranded ship in thirsting force. As my old friend the late Alasdair Alpin MacGregor (a crusading teetotaller) wrote: 'thereby hangs a tale of orgy and drunkenness surpassing any in the history of the Outer Hebrides.' It is a tale that has been wittily told by a non-teetotaller, the late Sir Compton Mackenzie, in *Whisky Galore*.

Johnnie Walker

One often wonders to what extent skilful advertising influences the public's choice of whisky; there are other factors apart from the contents of the bottle. White Horse sales doubled almost overnight when it became the first brand to introduce the screw-cap. And did Johnnie Walker derive its fame from what is certainly a most respected blend or from the slogan 'Johnnie Walker... Born 1820 still going strong'? In that year **John Walker** opened a shop selling groceries and wines and spirits in Kilmarnock. As time went on whisky became its main business and John's son Alexander took a big step forward by opening an office in London in 1880. It wasn't until after Alexander's death that the famous drawing depicting the spritely top-hatted figure with stick, quizzing glass, white breeches and leather riding boots appeared and the name of Johnnie Walker became one of the most famous in the field.

Ironically in April 1978 the Red Label version of this internationally best selling blend was removed from British shops due to pressure from the E.E.C. Its place has been taken by an almost identical product called 'John Barr', named after a Dufftown man who was a former managing director of the company. I notice no significant difference between Johnnie Walker Red Label and John Barr.

Vat 69

Another well known brand, still going strong after 96 years is Vat 69. The story goes that **William Sanderson**, a concoctor of alcoholic cordials in Leith, composed a hundred different blends of whisky and asked his friends to pick the one they liked the best. The majority chose the 69th vatting and Sanderson agreed with them.

Teacher's

Equally well-known in the blending world is Teacher's Highland Cream, a whisky of such excellence that in a blind tasting held in January 1978 in London the majority of the panel of connoisseurs rated it as a de luxe blend, not the standard and highly popular brand that it is.

William Teacher opened a dram shop in Glasgow in 1830 when he was only 19; before long he had 18 shops and was the largest licence holder in the city. In 1884 he registered his

Highland Cream and today it sells over a million bottles a week throughout the world.

A survey conducted by National Opinion Polls between 1973 and 1975 revealed that Teacher's was asked for by more whisky drinkers than any other brand (but see 1977 U.K. sales figures on p 41). The company, which is now part of Allied Breweries, owns Ardmore and Glendronach distilleries and its chairman is a direct descendant of the original founder.

Grant's

A late starter in the whisky field but a firm which now outsells every other as far as single malt is concerned and whose blended whisky is highly successful is William Grant & Sons. **William Grant** got his first job as a book-keeper at a distillery; he became manager of Mortlach and in 1886 with the help of his seven sons built the Glenfiddich distillery. Five years later he built a second one, Balvenie. The history since then has been one of continuous expansion and the firm, which is still privately owned, is one of the most successful in Scotland — in 1974 Glenfiddich became the first malt distillery to win the Queen's Award for Export Achievement.

Mackinlay's

Another family which has distinguished itself in the relatively short annals of blended whisky are the **Mackinlays.** 'From father to son over five generations,' is their proud advertising boast; the present production director is Donald Mackinlay and although the firm was bought by Scottish and Newcastle Breweries in 1962 the magic of the Mackinlay name remains on the bottle.

Courtyard of Miltonduff distillery, Elgin

A Taste of Scotch

In wine-growing countries there are, according to folk myth, Super Palates who can detect not only the vineyard of origin but the corner from which the grapes came and, as the joke goes, the kind of scissors the bunches were cut with. Are there Super Noses in Scotland?

'That's a question only someone from outside the industry would ask,' a blender replied. 'We're not in the business of identifying which little distillery a malt comes from, only if it's right and correct for the blend.'

All blenders can tell their own blend without any trouble but most of them would be hard put to identify more than a few rival blends in a blind tasting. 'An occupational hazard for a blender,' one told me, 'is the know-all in the pub who comes up to you with a dram and says "go on, you're the expert, tell me whose brand that is." I could tell him whether I thought it was better than my own blend or not, but I try to avoid encounters like that.'

Stuart Lang of Lang Brothers lamented the fact that 'there's not as much palate appreciation as we would like to think there is. A lot of people order a brand because it's fashionable, not because they are able to detect subtle differences of origin. We had one man who retired a few months ago, Jack Maclean, a teetotaller, our sample room manager. He didn't like doing it but I've seen him nose ten proprietary brands blind and get seven or eight right, but he would only do it as a non-publicity thing.'

Not so long ago a Scottish television programme invited a panel of experts along to a blind tasting and a lot of them pronounced Cameron Brig grain whisky to be a lovely Speyside malt!

What to Take with Blends

I have listed a few of the traditional ways of taking blended whisky and some of the downright unpleasant in an Appendix. I have never been a party to the adulteration of champagne with Guinness, orange juice or brandy — they are four excellent drinks

in their own right and should be enjoyed on their own. So with
whisky, either pot still or blended — the right and proper way to
take it is diluted with as soft and pure a water as you can find. In
Italy they lace it with soda water, in the States they drink it frozen
on the rocks, but how do they drink it in Scotland? That surely
must be the correct way? I have to report, with little enthusiasm,
that the Scots frequently lace it with fizzy lemonade and wash it
down with half a pint of beer. 'It's a shame when you put so much
time and trouble into creating a really harmonious blend that it
should be treated like that.' I agree with the head blender who
made that remark. There are even more eccentric combinations:
the Crown Hotel in Stornoway in the Isle of Lewis serves a £3
cocktail called Jelly Beans which consists of whisky, gin, vodka,
Pernod, cherry brandy, Babycham and lemonade.

Where and When to Drink Scotch

Ideally of course Scotch should be tasted in the Highlands, and
preferably in the open air, to the sound of distant pipes. It is
mandatory with haggis on Burns Night (January 25th) and
comforting with honey when fevered with a cold. There are those
who would say that there are few occasions when a good dram
would be out of place; a sentiment expressed by one of my
favourite pseudonymous authors, the 'Governor', who published
an account of his yachting holidays in the Hebrides in 1879.
Commenting on the possible ill effects that might be brought on
by the dampness encountered in those parts he suggested that:

> 'Any anticipated evil may usually be averted by the judicious use of the
> not unpalatable wine of the country, diluted to the taste or capacity of
> the user. This beverage is as appropriate a concomitant of a humid
> climate as the soothing dock is of the irritating nettle, and the same
> benificent Providence doubtless arranges the mutual proximity in
> either case.
>
> 'It is impossible to lay down absolute rules as to when this valuable
> therapeutic agent may be partaken of with advantage; but it may be
> suggested that about noon each day a moderate quantum should be
> served out with twice its bulk of water added.
>
> 'Before dinner it will be found an admirable stimulant to the
> appetite, or if that is already voracious, it will temper it to a gentle
> craving. During dinner it supplies the requisite fluid element of the
> meal; and after dinner a modest sip undoubtedly assists digestion.
> Between meals it will rouse the flagging energies, and it is as certainly
> an excellent promoter of the feast of reason at the evening chat as it is
> the best possible nightcap.'

Scotch — Luxury or Necessity?

The Scots have more than ample reason to rebel against the
discriminatory amounts of duty levelled on their national drink.

The Englishman's beer and cider are subject to a far lower duty in comparison with their alcoholic content; even foreign table and fortified wines do better. Since the end of World War Two duty on whisky has risen from less than a pound to £3.16 a bottle and the duty levied per degree of alcoholic strength in midsummer 1978 works out like this:

Beer	8.59p
British fortified wine	11.84p
Imported sherry	12.62p
Imported table wine	16.25p
Scotch whisky	27.09p

When you translate these figures into the duty the drinker pays for comparable amounts of alcohol in those five beverages the discrimination against Scotch is demonstrated even more clearly:

½ pint Beer	3.73p duty
2 oz British fortified wine	4.69p
2 oz imported Sherry	5.52p
3½ oz imported table wine	7.11p
1 oz Scotch Whisky	11.85p

Effectively Scotch has been priced out of the everyday reach of many Scots who pay thrice the duty on their whisky the Englishman pays on his bitter. The sad fact that alcoholism has been described as the Scottish Sickness and the incidence of drunkenness, absenteeism, indeed mortality due to drink is higher in Scotland than any other part of Britain, might make the substantial taxes levied on whisky by successive Chancellors of the Exchequer look more like an attempt at curbing potential excess than just mere Sassenach spite.

A point of view I put to a whisky executive, whose theory is that alcohol causes alcoholics, not whisky. 'Relatively few people drink whisky neat and in fact most people put so much water with it that it is far weaker than wine. If you see a drunk lying on the pavement in Glasgow it's not a bottle of whisky he's got in his pocket but something much cheaper.'

Beer is included in the Cost of Living Index and whisky isn't; beer is regarded as a working man's drink and working men vote with their elbows; beer has been treated more gingerly than Scotch — the drink of West End clubs not East End pubs. That is maybe the English way of looking at things. But when a Scot wishes to drink your health it's with a dram of whisky, not a can of beer. And the Scots claim that these punitive rates of taxation make it increasingly difficult for them to sell whisky overseas. 'If a salesman had to sell a Mini for £8,600 he'd find it impossible,' says Adam Bergius, Chairman of Teacher's, 'but that's what a Mini would cost if it were bearing the same rate of duty on value as Scotch does.'

Overseas finance ministers keep a watchful eye on 11 Downing Street and when British Chancellors increase domestic duty on whisky, as they have done ten times since 1947, it makes life immediately more difficult for whisky exporters. 'We export to 87 countries over £500 million worth of whisky a year and whenever Scotch is penalised yet again in Britain,' a whisky man complained, 'it's an inspiration to every foreign finance minister to do the same. The last time the British Chancellor increased the tax on whisky, 79 finance ministers followed suit within a few months.'

Because whisky has now become something of a luxury, supermarket chains have adopted new strategies to sell it. The standard 75 cl bottle has been reduced in size to 70 cl and the standard strength has been reduced from 70° proof to 65.5° — few shoppers have noticed anything but the reduction in price.

If and when Scotland does achieve a degree of autonomy there'll be a great clamour for an immediate reduction in the duty on their national drink; a move which could put back the clock in the Borders to the days when there was a rigid Excise control between Scotland and England. Graham Smith, the Librarian and Archivist of H.M. Customs and Excise, has drawn my attention to the special Border Service which was authorised in 1830 when the duty on Spirits was only 3s 4d a proof gallon in Scotland but 7s 6d in England.

Sixty officers were employed 'in traversing and watching the roads by which smugglers travel.' They were cautioned to be 'well armed and mounted and (to) abstain from drinking to excess.' When the railway line between Edinburgh and Newcastle was opened in 1846, passengers had to submit to the indignity of having their baggage examined upon arriving at Berwick and Carlisle railway stations. A correspondent complained in *The Times* that the country was becoming 'a minor European principality with annoying and petty border restrictions.'

I'm quite sure that if independence arrived for Scotland and the situation arose again few Scots would find it at all annoying or petty to pay less for whisky than their English neighbours. With Burns to a man, they'd cry: 'Whisky and freedom gang thegither.'

Tasting Malt Whisky

There are only two ways to enjoy malt whisky fully — at the strength it is presented to you in bottle, or diluted to what you consider suitable. Diluted not with over-chlorinated recycled effluent but as neutral and as soft water as you can obtain.

If you are lucky enough to live in the Highlands — or indeed in Glasgow where the city supply comes soft from Loch Katrine — you'll have no problems but if your piped supply is unpleasant it is worth buying bottled water; one not too heavy with minerals and *not* gaseous. Sparkling water added to malt whisky does not improve it at all, neither does the addition of carbonated water.

There are people who prefer to drink a 70° proof malt neat, regarding it as reduced enough already. For after-dinner drinking this is a sensible way to approach it but as an aperitif (if you are among those who regard spirits as an acceptable prelude to a meal) then a splash of water will unlock all the aromas latent in the whisky.

If you watch blenders at work you will see them select a tulip-shaped glass and nose their malts reduced with water — the water releases the body of the spirit, the glass contains it and channels it upwards for olfactory appreciation.

Blenders, who have to sample up to two hundred malt and grain whiskies a day when they are working, seldom taste them. The whisky is only 'nosed'. If you start tasting whisky the palate soon becomes too immobilised for really objective appraisal. So 'nose' your whisky first and relish what it has to reveal: the flavour of the peat, the flavour of the cereal. Hold the glass up to the light and swirl the contents so that the whisky circles to the rim; you will see an oily deposit clinging to the sides of the glass. The heavier the malt the heavier and more viscous as it falls.

As the glass warms in your hand, more of the subtle flavours will be released and you may detect the phenols imparted by the peat when the malt was being dried and other fragrances which may, if you have a romantic strain in you, conjure up visions of heathery glens and peat-brown burns.

Taste the whisky neat and then add a little water. I have heard people claim that they can detect the taste of seaweed in some of the Islay malts; there is certainly an almost medicinal quality, a hint of iodine in a malt like Laphroaig, but I don't think it has anything to do with the distillery's stance on the edge of the sea.

Some people think the really pungent Islay malts too heavy and oily. In the early days a lot of blenders found them too forceful and as Barnard pointed out in the 1890s in his paper *How To Blend Scotch Whisky* 'Some years ago a prejudice rose against (Islay) whisky, owing to its being so fat, and many inexperienced blenders using it too freely and too young, but of late years its use has been better understood, and, besides, the whisky is more carefully made, the flavour being more delicate and less pungent, owing to the use of dry peats instead of damp ones for drying the malt.' The nineteenth century Islays must have filled a room with peat-reek when the cork was drawn.

And it wasn't only the after-taste of peat that arrested your attention. George Saintsbury*, sometime Professor of Rhetoric and English Literature at Edinburgh University, noted that over

* Saintsbury, critic and literary historian, was born in 1845 and published his famous *Notes on a Cellar Book* in 1920.

the 45 years in which he had been taking an informed interest in malt whisky the general style had undergone a change: 'the older whiskies were darker in colour, from being kept in golden sherry or madeira casks, rather than sweeter in taste, and rather heavier in texture; the newer are "lighter" in both the first and the last respect, and much drier in taste. But the abominable tyranny of enforced "breaking down" to thirty below proof has spoilt the ethers of the older whiskies terribly.'

It is only if you have the good fortune to be offered a 'small sensation' in a distillery manager's office that you will be able to admire a whisky in its unreduced state.

There is something about a really powerful malt whisky taken in its birthplace along with a moistening of its native burn or spring water which cannot be re-created anywhere else.

Perhaps whisky is not a good traveller; perhaps it needs, like many a wine, to be drunk on the spot. I find I enjoy drinking Talisker far more in Skye than I do anywhere else. Just as ouzo and retsina are best taken in the warmth of the Greek islands, so Talisker and Lagavulin and Bruichladdich lose something when you wrench them from the far and frequently moist and windy Hebrides. But maybe that's just fancy.

As to the optimum age this very much depends on circumstances. David Daiches had the rare fortune to drink, at Longmorn distillery near Elgin, whisky from a cask that was filled four years after the distillery was built in 1895 and not broached until 1967: 'By all the rules it should have gone "woody" — and indeed, it should have evaporated, because a loss of 2 per cent per annum over eighty-eight years should yield less than nothing. But in fact it was not woody at all: it had lost strength and body, but it was mellow and pleasant though (surprisingly perhaps) without the character of a much younger Longmorn.'

All who enjoy malt whiskies will have their favourites. Just as the industry has never got together to systematise the descriptions that may be applied to whisky, so there has been no attempt to categorise malts in the way that the wines of Bordeaux were given their rigid orders of merit in 1855.

It has been generally accepted that Smith's Glenlivet is first in more ways than one. At one time over two dozen distilleries on Speyside covering an area of 300 square miles had associated themselves with Glenlivet by hyphenage; among them Macallan, Longmorn, Glenrothes, Aberlour, Glenburgie, Glenkeith, Glen Moray, Glen Spey, Miltonduff, Strathisla, Tamnavulin and Tomintoul. Such was the cachet of Smith's Glenlivet that in 1880 Colonel John Gordon Smith took legal proceedings and secured the sole right to use 'The Glenlivet' as his trade name.

Lists have been made of course, but they are very personal things. Of the malts ready to hand in hotel bars I find Glenmorangie perhaps the most acceptable as an easy-to-appreciate malt whisky. It is mellow without being bland and has both aroma and bouquet — a malt to enjoy after a hard day in the open and a hot bath in one of those Highland shooting lodge hotels where the Victorian brass fittings are only outstripped by the Oregon pine panelling. I would suggest it every time as an introduction for anyone who has never tried a single malt before.

With Glenmorangie I would place Glenfiddich, more universally available overseas than any other single malt, and therefore the one which I have been offered more than most. Familiarity has bred respect.

For sheer panache I'd bracket Laphroaig, Talisker and Highland Park next. Islay, Skye and Orkney produce them and they have the individuality found in islands and the slight idiosyncratic wildness. Just as marc is to cognac so are these three malts to the more urbane whiskies of Speyside.

The Glenlivet, Glen Grant, Macallan, Longmorn . . . you must make your own list of Highland preferment and a lot will depend on your own preferences for small and special parts of the Scottish landscape. Its not perhaps just an idle thought that whiskies are very much part of their environment. Perhaps I favour Talisker because it was the first distillery I ever saw in operation. I remember as a child feeling the heat of the coal furnaces beneath the stills and the sweet sour smell of the mash. And if I come across a bottle of Talisker in an alien bar then a dram of it puts me firmly back on Skye.

Just as there is a right time for Cognac so there is a right and proper time for the really outstanding malts. As Neil Gunn puts it: 'the perfect moment for their reception is after arduous bodily stress — or mental stress, if the body be sound. The essential oils that wind in the glass then uncurl their long fingers in lingering benediction and the nobler works of Creation are made manifest.'

As you can see it is a spirit which leads you into hyperbole before you know what's hit you. I remember some years ago being pole-axed by hyperbole myself when confronted with a particularly potent dram of Talisker in the old distillery on the seaweed tangled shores of Loch Harport:

> 'I am offered a sample of the almost colourless liquid. It is spirited enough to power a jet fighter. The pungent, slightly oily, peaty ruggedness of the bouquets mounts into my nostrils. The corpus of the drink advances like the lava of the Cuillins down my throat. Then voom! Steam rises from the temples, a seismic shock rocks the building, my eyes are seen to water, cheeks aflame I steady myself against a chair. Talisker is not a drink, it is an interior explosion, distilled central heating; it depth-charges the parts, bangs doors and slams windows. There's nothing genteel about Talisker'.*

Obviously one of those occasions when it might have been better if words had failed one.

* *Hebridean Connection* (Routledge, 1977)

9

Visiting the Distilleries

Just as Scotch is synonymous with Scotland, so its distilleries, some of them dating back to the 18th century, many of them well over a century old, represent the country's most tangible commercial link with the past.

In many areas, indeed, the distillery is the only working relic of a pre-industrial age. Other crafts have atrophied: wheelwrights, waggonmakers, cordwainers, farriers, weavers have all gone. The buildings where a score of manual skills were practised have either been pulled down or converted to other uses.

Although microprocessors may have replaced muscle-power, many distilleries present an external face remarkably unchanged by time. The stillman may be pressing buttons but the alchemy that converts barley into whisky is an historic one, frequently performed in buildings that are themselves a part of history.

It is only fairly recently that distilleries have opened their doors to those unconnected with the trade and there are still many which do not have organised facilities for receiving visitors. Some may take on a student in the summer months to show tourists round; others, realising the potential goodwill that a guided tour engenders, have provided special reception centres, museums and exhibitions and welcome all comers with enthusiasm.

There are distilleries which are too cramped to show the public round with comfort and at these you may get a polite refusal. The best advice, if you are going to be touring in the vicinity of a distillery, is to find out either from the local tourist office or from your hotel how welcome you might be, or to telephone the local manager. Bear in mind that these days there are few people involved in running a distillery: during the week they are all busy men and women — taking an hour off to show you round can make a big hole in their day.

Remember, too, that although the old 'silent season' has largely disappeared, most distilleries close for their annual holiday and maintenance in the summer months and in July and August you may well find no distilling taking place.

The following distilleries do have either visitor centres or special facilities for showing people round, on an *ad hoc* basis or by appointment. Other distilleries not on this list frequently accept parties if reasonable warning is given. So if you're near a distillery not mentioned here, try on the off-chance anyway!

Auchentoshan	Glenmorangie
Balvenie	Glenugie
Blair Athol	Highland Park
Bowmore	Inverleven
Dalmore	Ladyburn
Girvan	Miltonduff
Glen Albyn	Pulteney
Glendronach	Strathisla
Glenfarclas	Strathmill
Glenfiddich	Talisker
Glengarioch	Tamdhu
Glengoyne	Tomatin
Glen Grant	Tullibardine
Glen Mhor	

Many distilleries are tucked away in secluded glens and may be difficult to find but once in an area like Speyside you'll soon be able to detect the characteristic pagoda-kiln and the chimneys which reveal the presence of a distillery. In recent years, new landmarks have been added in the shape of the tall evaporating towers where the pot ale is mixed with the spent grain from the mash and dried out as cattle cake pellets.

There is only one 'Whisky Trail' in Scotland and that has been mapped out by the Department of Leisure, Recreation and Tourism in the Grampian Region where 60 distilleries are located. The trail, which visits Glenfiddich, Balvenie, Glenfarclas, Tamdhu and Strathisla, is 62 miles long and can take from four to six hours depending on how many distilleries you stop at. The tour takes in the whisky village of Tomintoul, one of the highest in Scotland, and the big whisky centre of Dufftown.

GAZETTEER

This section lists the malt distilleries of Scotland in alphabetical order, followed by the grain distilleries. Some of the more interesting features of their history and situation are described, but many of them have far more to interest the reader than can be shown in this necessarily brief survey. The numbers in brackets after each entry refer to their location on the maps on pages 00-000.

Malt distilleries are distinguished as Campbeltown (**C**), Highland (**H**), Islay (**I**), and Lowland (**L**).

Key to Map of Scottish Malt Distilleries *(opposite)*

Lowland Malt

1 Auchentoshan	5 Kinclaith	9 Rosebank
2 Bladnoch	6 Ladyburn	10 St. Magdalene
3 Glenkinchie	7 Littlemill	11 Moffat
4 Inverleven	8 Lomond	

Islay Malt

12 Ardbeg	15 Bunnahabhain	18 Laphroaig
13 Bowmore	16 Caol Ila	19 Port Ellen
14 Bruichladdich	17 Lagavulin	

Campbeltown Malt

34 Glen Scotia	35 Springbank

Highland Malt
(For the distilleries in the Speyside inset see page 79)

36 Aberfeldy	69 Glendronach	109 Lochnagar
38 Ardmore	129 Glen Foyle	98 Lochside
40 Balblair	127 Glengarioch	101 Macduff
43 Banff	74 Glenglassaugh	102 Millburn
44 Ben Nevis	75 Glengoyne	105 North Port
47 Benromach	124 Glenlochy	126 Oban
48 Ben Wyvis	79 Glenlossie	106 Ord
49 Blair Athol	80 Glen Mhor	107 Pulteney
52 Clynelish	81 Glenmorangie	108 Royal Brackla
58 Dallas Dhu	86 Glenturret	110 Scapa
59 Dalmore	87 Glenugie	128 Speyside
60 Dalwhinnie	88 Glenury-Royal	114 Talisker
61 Deanston	89 Highland Park	117 Teaninich
63 Edradour	90 Hillside	123 Tobermory
64 Fettercairn	93 Isle of Jura	118 Tomatin
65 Glen Albyn	95 Knockdhu	121 Tullibardine
68 Glencadam	97 Loch Lomond	

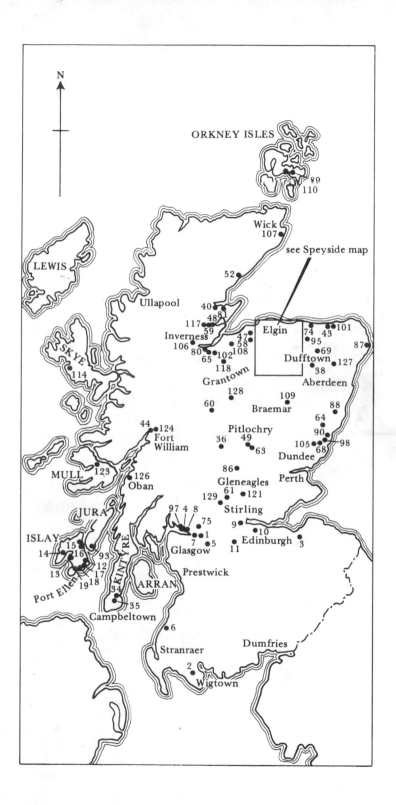

Aberfeldy   Perthshire. **H** (36)

This attractive little town on the River Tay is notable for its fine
five-span bridge, built at the behest of General Wade in 1773 by
William Adam. The distillery is on the outskirts of the town on the
A827. It was built in 1896 by 'Whisky Tom' Dewar near his
father's birthplace to take the place of Tulliemet distillery, south-
east of Pitlochry, which the company had leased from the Duke of
Atholl. There is an active cooperage and although a new still
house was built in 1972 the familiar outline of the old pagoda-
roofed maltings has been retained.

Aberlour-Glenlivet   Aberlour, Banffshire. **H** (37)

Built in 1826 at the foot of Ben Rinnes on the banks of the Lour, a
tributary of the Spey, by one James Grant. The distillery was
renovated in 1880 and at that time all the grinding, mashing,
elevating and pumping was driven by waterpower. The original
village was called Charlestown of Aberlour after its founder
Charles Grant of Wester Elchies who laid it out in 1812. It stands
on the site of a church dedicated in the sixth century to St.
Drostan the Pictish saint, and Drostan's Well lies in the distillery
grounds. The distillery was enlarged in 1973. Its whisky goes
largely for blending but is also bottled at nine years old and 70
proof.

Aberlour-Glenlivet Distillery

Allta'Bhainne   Dufftown, Banffshire. **H** (131)

Built by Chivas Bros, a subsidiary of Seagrams of Canada, the
buildings are of local granite and are slated traditionally.
Although no malting occurs, there is an architectural nod towards
the past with the inclusion in the design of four small pagoda
roofs. The complex is automated, button controlled and designed
so that production can be doubled if that proves necessary. By
mid-1978 the distillery had produced 1.5 million gallons of
whisky, none of which will be used before 1980.

Ardbeg Islay. **I** (12)

Independently owned, the distillery was legally established in 1815 on the site of an extensive illlicit operation. Barnard describes how, having been searched out by the Revenue men and their equipment seized, the traffickers disbanded and migrated to the shores of Kintyre. The water supply still comes from Lochs Uigidale and Arinambeast. Ardbeg malts its own barley and flavours it with locally cut peat. Although most of the output goes for blending it is bottled at 10 years old and at 80 proof.

Ardbeg Distillery

Ardmore Kennethmont, 7 miles south of Huntly in north west Aberdeenshire. **H** (38)

Built by William Teacher in 1898; the malt is still used exclusively by Teachers in blending their noted 'Highland Cream,' a brand name first registered in 1884. The distillery takes its water from the Knockando Hill and the steam engine which once powered the works is still on the site. There is a handsome pyramid-shaped kiln. A little to the north lies Leith Hall, owned by the National Trust for Scotland.

Auchentoshan Old Kilpatrick, Strathclyde. **L** (1)

Founded just south of the Highland line in 1825 and lying about ten miles north of Glasgow. The product is marketed as a single malt at 70 proof. Water supply is drawn from the Kilpatrick hills which are north of the Highland line. About a mile away are the remains of a Roman fort and part of the Antonine wall. The whisky is triple distilled in a wash still, a low wines still and a spirit still, a 15 hour operation which lends a lightness to the taste and is only found in one other distillery, Springbank.

Auchroisk   Mulben, Banffshire. **H** (122)

This to my mind is one of the most elegant and graceful new distilleries in Scotland; the detailing and the workmanship are superb. Excluding the warehouses it cost a million pounds. On the site almost all I.D.V.'s numerous fillings of Speyside malt whiskies are aged. Whisky from other distilleries is collected by road tanker and filled into cask for maturing. The seven warehouses have a capacity of more than ten million gallons and Auchroisk is now the administrative centre for I.D.V.'s other Highland distilleries, Glen Spey, Strathmill and Knockando. The output capacity is 1½ million proof gallons a year. Housed here is the Victorian steam engine which used to mill grain at Strathmill. Work began on the complex in 1974 and as in all the postwar distilleries manpower is minimal; all is electronic and functional. Nine men operate a 24-hour shift cycle.

Aultmore   Keith, Banffshire. **H** (39)

Sited in the centre of what was once a notorious area of illicit whisky bothies. When the outlying districts were visited from time to time by preventive officers, white cloths about two yards square would be placed on peat stacks as a warning that trouble was in the offing. The illicit spirit was in great demand by hotel-keepers in Keith, Fochabers and Portgordon. The distillery was completed in 1896 and is now owned by Scottish Malt Distillers, a subsidiary of D.C.L. The product is mainly used for blending but is also bottled at 12 years old and 70 proof. Aultmore was one of the 23 distilleries which added the distinction of Glenlivet to its name when it was built.

Balblair   Edderton, Tain, Ross-shire. **H** (40)

It is possible that men were fermenting ale on this site as early as 1749 but distilling did not begin until 1842. The distillery lies about a quarter of a mile from Dornoch Firth in what used to be known as the Parish of Peats, and the barley is still malted in the traditional way. Professor McDowall suggests that the slightly aromatic flavour of the whisky which is bottled at 10 years old and 70 proof may be due to this local friable peat.

Balmenach   Cromdale, Grantown-on-Spey. **H** (41)

When Barnard visited the distillery in the 1880s by train, although the line had been open for 20 years 'we were the only persons who had ever booked to Cromdale first class, the number of our tickets, which were faded with age, commencing at ought.' On arrival they were taken to see the former haunts of smugglers

who abounded in the region, one of whom, an illicit distiller
called James Macgregor, took out a licence in 1824. Barnard and
his companion tasted some 1873 whisky and 'found it prime, and
far superior in our opinion to old brandy. Some of the whisky was
supplied by desire to the proprietor of the Gairloch Hotel,
Lochmaree, in 1878, for the special use of Her Majesty the Queen
and her suite.' In those days there was a farm of 1200 acres
attached to the distillery and 100 head of cattle were fed on the
waste draff. The floor maltings were replaced by Saladin
mechanical maltings in 1964.

Balvenie   Dufftown, Banffshire. **H** (42)

Balvenie was built in 1892 with stones retrieved from New
Balvenie castle which William Grant, owner of nearby
Glenfiddich, bought for £200. Like Glenfiddich it draws its water
supply from a secret spring, the Robbie Dubh, and visitors are
able to see the malting floors in operation. There is a reception
centre and visitors are welcome from Monday to Friday, 10.30 to
12.30 and 2 to 4.30. Balvenie is available at eight years old and 70
proof. Although the same water and the same malt are used for
both Balvenie and Glenfiddich (indeed Balvenie supplies malt for
Glenfiddich) the two whiskies are recognisably different. Balvenie
is lower down the hill than its older brother which may have
something to do with the difference, but more likely the
distinctions occur in the stills. Balvenie has a vapour chamber
round the waist while at Glenfiddich the stills have lamp glass and
ball type heads.

Banff   Mill of Banff, one mile from Banff. **H** (43)

At the mouth of the Deveron, Banff is one of the most attractive
towns in the north of Scotland. A Royal Burgh and a holiday
resort, it contains Duff House, one of the most splendid Adam
buildings in existence. The distillery was established in 1824. In
1863 it was rebuilt on a new site and, after a fire, reconstructed in
1877. It was bombed during the last war and now its entire
production goes into the D.C.L. blends.

Ben Nevis   Lochy Bridge, Fort William. **H** (44)

When Alexander Smith, author of *A Summer in Skye,* visited the
distillery in the 1860s he took a letter of introduction to Long John
Macdonald the owner: 'This gentleman was the tallest man I ever
beheld and must in his youth have been of incomparable
physique. I presented my letter and was received with the
hospitality and courteous grace so characteristic of the old Gael.
He is gone now, the happy hearted Hercules — gone like one of

his own drams.' Long John built the distillery in 1825 and he lived to present a cask of whisky to Queen Victoria on one of her visits to Fort William in April 1848: 'An order has been sent to the Treasury to permit the spirits to be removed to the cellars of Buckingham Palace,' the *Illustrated London News* reported, 'free of duty. The cask is not be opened until His Royal Highness the Prince of Wales attains his majority.' And that was 15 years later when the Dew of Ben Nevis, as Long John called his malt, would have been at its peak. His famous name is perpetuated in the Long John Distilleries. Ben Nevis is both a malt and grain distillery and still produces Dew of Ben Nevis.

Ben Nevis Distillery

Benriach-Glenlivet   Longmorn, Elgin, Morayshire. **H** (45)

In many ways an ill-fated distillery, Benriach was built in 1894 and closed in 1903 when the whisky bubble burst and a recession set in. Along with Caperdonich, Benriach was rebuilt and reopened in 1965. Its whisky is used for blending in such brands as Queen Anne, Something Special, and St. Leger.

Benrinnes   Aberlour. **H** (46)

The distillery was built in 1835 and is planted on the eastern slopes of Ben Rinnes 1030 feet above sea level. The site was selected for its water, which rises from springs on the summit of the mountain and, as Barnard noted, 'can be seen on a clear day some miles distant, sparkling over the prominent rocks on its downward course, passing over mossy banks and gravel, which perfectly filters it before it reaches the Distillery.' The stills were built on the small side to produce a rich thick spirit. Because of its cool high position, work in the old days, when barley was malted in the distillery, went on all through the summer, which was unusual at the time. A major reconstruction took place in 1955, when the floor maltings were replaced by Saladin boxes.

Benromach   Forres, Morayshire. **H** (47)

Built in 1898, the distillery is now owned by D.C.L.

Ben Wyvis   Invergordon. **H** (48)

Opened in 1965 by Invergordon Distillers, the malt distillery is overshadowed by the huge grain distillery on the same site. Named after the mountain which dominates the area, the company tell me that the whisky is 'of fine character and flavour worthy to take its place alongside the great highland malts.' It forms a constituent part of Findlater's Finest Whisky.

Ben Wyvis Distillery

Bladnoch   Bladnoch, Wigtownshire. **L** (2)

The distillery lies on the banks of the river Bladnoch about a mile from the county town of one of the most unvisited and therefore unspoiled parts of Scotland. It has the distinction of being the southernmost distillery in Scotland. Its malt is available at 70 proof. It would be an interesting experiment to compare the present dram with the pre-war. Bladnoch was closed for 18 years and didn't come back into production until the mid-fifties.

Blair Athol. H (49)

Thirty miles north of Perth in the pretty little tourist town of Pitlochry with its summer festival theatre, salmon river and

Edwardian hydro hotels is a distillery, part of which has stood there for more than 200 years. Going north you pass Macbeth's Birnam wood and the ancient town of Dunkeld. The distillery was established in 1826 by a Mr Connacher who was said to be a descendant of the chivalrous young Conacher, admirer of the legendary Fair Maid of Perth. Illicit whisky was distilled round Pitlochry for generations. 'Doubtless,' records the invaluable Barnard, 'it was the mellow barley bree* from the caverns of Ben Vrackie that warmed the hearts and strengthened the arms of the Highlanders at Killiecrankie and which enabled them to rout the Southerns from the pass.' The burn of Allt Dour (The Burn of the Otter) runs through the distillery and in the nineteenth century the malt was dried with peat bought from Orkney. Distilling was abandoned for quite a time and it wasn't until after the 1939-45 war that Arthur Bell & Sons refurbished the place and began distilling once again. It has a reception centre.

Bowmore   Islay. **I** (13)

The distillery was established in 1779 which makes it the legally oldest in Islay. Still using its floor maltings, the distillery has a reception centre commanding sea views and a small museum of distilling bygones. The whisky, made from the waters of the River Laggan, is bottled at 70 proof and 8 years old.

Bowmore Distillery

Brackla   *see* Royal Brackla

Braes of Glenlivet   Banffshire. **H** (132)
Built in 1973 the distillery has a traditional pagoda-shaped
* broth

skyline, white harled walls and blue slated roofs. By 1978 it had already made four million proof gallons of whisky and its annual output, worth £3 million, is produced with the help of highly automated engineering by only five men. The stills are based on the shape of those at Strathisla, another Chivas Bros. distillery. It is perhaps a sad comment on society's ability to organise itself that in an area of Britain which has a high rate of unemployment, increasing production means not increasing the number of jobs but drastically reducing them. The first whisky for such blends as 100 Pipers and Passport was drawn from the warehouses in September 1978.

Brora   *See* Clynelish

Bruichladdich   Islay. **I** (14)

A long low-lying complex on the shores of Loch Indaal opposite Bowmore distillery two miles from Port Charlotte and 6 from Bridgend, built in 1881. Its water supply has always come by pipeline from a reservoir in the interior. This may account for its notable mildness as compared with the massive peaty assault of Laphroaig. The distillery (which no longer does its own malting) was modernised in 1960 without altering its traditional aspect and is owned by Invergordon Distillers. 'The distillery manager and his staff,' I am told, 'welcome opportunities to show visitors round Bruichladdich and to pour them a dram or two of the splendid whisky which they make there.' Bruichladdich, the most westerly of all the Scottish distilleries, has a capacity of 450,000 proof gallons and bottles its own malt at 75 proof and 5 years old.

Bruichladdich Distillery, from the sea

Bunnahabhain   Islay. **I** (15)

Like all the other distilleries on Islay, in the old days all the links
with the outside world were seawards. Barley and coal came in to
the wooden pier which is still there, and the barrels were taken by
steamer up the Clyde to Glasgow. The distillery, built in 1881,
commands a fine view of the celebrated Paps of Jura. Its malt can
be tasted in the 'Famous Grouse' blend produced by Highland
Distilleries.

Caol Ila   Islay, north of Port Askaig. **I** (16)

The distillery was built in 1846 on the shores of the narrow Sound
of Jura. The descent to the distillery is still a steep one and
although there was rebuilding in 1974 when production was
doubled, Caol Ila remains externally largely unchanged. No
malting is carried out on the site, all supplies coming from the
D.C.L.'s central maltings in Port Ellen. The staff of 29 produce
20,000 gallons of whisky a week. The whisky has been put on the
Italian market as a single malt but the bulk goes for blending.

Caol Ila Distillery

Caperdonich   Rothes, Morayshire. **H** (50)

When this distillery was built just across the road from Glen Grant
in 1897 it was known as Glen Grant No.2. As demand for whisky
slackened it was closed a few years later and was not rebuilt and
reopened until 1965 when it was given its new name, which in
Gaelic means 'The Secret Well'. Push-button operated, the
distillery has stainless steel washbacks and malt is bought in. I
have not tasted Caperdonich but although it uses water from the
same burn as Glen Grant, its whisky is said to be lighter.

Cardow Knockando, Morayshire. **H** (51)

Cardow was licensed in 1824 in an area hotching with smugglers who transported their casks over the Mannoch Hill to Elgin and Forres. From the hill came both good peat and clear sparkling burn water. The first licensed distiller was a John Cumming, great-grandfather of Sir Ronald Cumming, who became chairman of D.C.L. John was succeeded by his son, whose widow carried on the business for many years, the only woman distiller of her day. In the early days the whisky was taken by horse and cart to Burghead on the coast, now the site of giant new maltings, and then sailed round to Leith. In 1884 the distillery was moved 300 yards to its present site, and nine years later Mrs Cumming sold out to John Walker & Sons. Reconstruction in 1960 boosted the capacity (when distilling began again in April 1961) to 320,000 gallons a year; the single malt, known as Cardhu, is sold at 70 proof and 12 years.

Clynelish Brora, Sutherland. **H** (52)

North of Brora, the old distillery was part of the notorious Duke of Sutherland's master plan to improve his enormous Highland estates, and provide a legitimate outlet for the local barley. At Brora, a new village was created; skilled men were imported to mine coal and labour at manufactures. The prohibition of illicit distilling had, according to the Duke's factor, James Loch, 'deprived a large class of the people of one of their most profitable sources of income.' The distillery built in 1819 used local coal and barley and employed 50 men. Clynelish was widely marketed in Victorian times and had a deservedly high reputation for its full flavour and fruitiness. For some extraordinary reason Scottish Malt distillers, the D.C.L. subsidiary which owns Clynelish, decided recently to transfer its name. So if you go to Sutherland to inspect the distillery of which dear old George Saintsbury wrote so fondly ask not for Clynelish but Brora! Clynelish today refers to a product of the new distillery built in 1967-8 on a site close to old Clynelish.

Coleburn Longmore, Elgin, Morayshire. **H** (53)

Built in 1896 in the Speyside area, the distillery is owned by D.C.L. and its whisky is used for blending.

Convalmore Dufftown, Banffshire. **H** (54)

One of the few malt distilleries to experiment with the patent still. One was installed in 1910 but the results were disappointing and it was removed during World War One. The distillery is owned by D.C.L. and all the output (which was doubled in 1964) goes for blending.

Cragganmore   Ballindalloch, Banffshire. **H** (55)

Lying in the heart of the mountains close to the Spey, the distillery
was built on the site of a smuggling bothy in 1869 and draws its
water supply from the Craggan burn. The output is used entirely
for blending by its owners D. & J. MacCallum and it can be
appreciated in their 'Perfection' blend and in other D.C.L.
whiskies.

Craigellachie   Craigellachie, Banffshire. **H** (56)

The town lies at the junction of the Fiddich and the Spey and is
one of the most beautiful in Morayshire. Noted for Thomas
Telford's dramatic iron bridge with its battlemented turrets, the
views of the Spey valley are spectacular. The distillery was built in
1890 and was, along with Lagavulin, the foundation for the
famous 'White Horse' blend created by the firm of James Logan
Mackie & Co. The distillery was bought by 'Restless Peter'
Mackie, the great salesman of White Horse, in 1915. The output
goes entirely for blending.

Dailuaine   Carron, Morayshire. **H** (57)

The distillery nestles in one of the most beautiful glens in Scotland
and it drove Barnard into ecstacies of prose: 'Never was there such
a soft, bright landscape of luxuriant green, of clustering foliage,
and verdant banks of wild flowers, ferns and grasses. The whole
scene is dainty enough for a fairy's palace and we do not wonder at
the choice of the ancient Queen, who, during the wars between
the Danes and the Scotch, selected Dail-uaine as a resting place,
and pitched her tents there as she journeyed to join her husband
after the battle of Mortlach.' Barnard was no less enchanted by
the distillery itself: 'Outside all is quiet and the stillness of death
reigns; inside it is all life, bustle and activity and the establishment
a little world of industry in itself. In this retired spot, far removed
from noisy cities and prying eyes, surrounded by all that is
beautiful and lovely in nature, is carried on the mystery of John
Barleycorn, — his death, burial and resurrection. No wonder
with these surroundings that the pure spirit emerging from such
an Eden should be appreciated by mortals all the world over.' The
distillery, built on the banks of the Carron burn which rises on
Ben Rinnes, is a handsome complex which includes the engine
shed for the distillery 'pug' which is preserved on the nearby
Strathspey private railway. If you ascend a slope above Dailuaine
you will be able to see a whole condensation of distilleries just as
Barnard did a hundred years before you: 'No less than seven —
The Glenlivet, Glenfarclas, Cragganmore, Cardow, Benrinnes,
Aberlour and Macallan, forming most of the celebrated Speyside

distilleries, Glen Rothes, Glen Spey, Glen Grant and Mortlach being hidden from our view by hills and woods.' The whisky is used for blending by its proprietors D.C.L. The floor maltings were closed in 1961 when 6 Saladin boxes were installed.

Dailuaine Distillery

Dallas Dhu   Forres, Morayshire. **H** (58)

Built in 1899, the distillery is virtually unchanged and apart from the fact that the barley is no longer malted on the spot a visit is rather like stepping back in time.

Dalmore   Alness, Ross-shire. **H** (59)

The distillery arose in 1839 on the site of an old meal mill and once had sole rights to the River Alness which flows into nearby Cromarty Firth. It commands splendid views of the Black Isle and does much of its own malting by the Saladin box process. In its earlier days its owners, the Mackenzie brothers, grew a large part of the barley needed and bred some noted Aberdeen Angus Polled cattle and pedigree Clydesdale horses. In those days the annual output was 80,000 gallons; today it is 1.2 million gallons and the cattle and horses are gone. The whisky is sold at 75 proof and 12 years old.

Dalwhinnie   Dalwhinnie. **H** (60)

A bleak and lonely hamlet high up on the main road between Perth and Inverness. The distillery which was built in 1898 is still in full production and is licensed to James Buchanan of 'Black and White' fame — yet another subsidiary of D.C.L.

Deanston   Doune. H (61)

In 1785 a cotton mill was built on the south bank of the River
Teith near Castle Doune in Perthshire. Designed by Richard
Arkwright, it was one of the first in Scotland. Its supply of pure
soft water from the Teith which had its headwaters in the
Trossachs proved ideal when, in 1965, cotton spinning was
discontinued and stills replaced the looms. The complex still looks
like a cotton mill but is now equipped to produce up to 750,000
gallons of whisky a year. Deanston Mill has lately been put on the
market as a single malt at 70 proof.

Dufftown-Glenlivet   Dufftown, Banffshire. H (62)

Dufftown is sometimes known, but surely only by newspaper
hacks, as the Golden City because so much whisky is stored there.
'Rome was built on seven hills,' runs an old couplet, 'Dufftown
stands on seven stills.' The distillery was built in Dullan Glen and
was bought by Bell's in 1933. Its water comes from a noted source
known as Jock's Well and the whisky, bottled as a single malt at 8
years old and 70 proof, is also used for blending in Bell's Extra
Special. See also Pittyvaich-Glenlivet.

Edradour   Pitlochry, Perthshire. H (63)

The smallest distillery in Scotland and surely one of the most
attractive. Built in 1837 at Balnauld near Pitlochry, it nestles at
the foot of a hill beside a steep-banked burn. It was powered by an
old water wheel until just after the end of World War Two and to
this day a staff of three turn out the weekly thousand gallons
which goes entirely into blending, notably 'House of Lords' and
'King's Ransom'. I remember talking many years ago to an old
man who had been in Barra at the time of the shipwreck of the
Politician (see page 50) and when I asked him which of all the
blends he sampled had impressed him most he had no second
thoughts: 'King's Ransom without a doubt!' Edradour has a
minute malt barn and kiln and its spirit still holds less than 300
gallons.

Fettercairn   Kincardineshire. H (64)

Fettercairn dates from the eighteenth century and has two
buildings of note nearby: Fettercairn House (1660) and Balbegno
Castle (1569). Its distillery, established in 1824, is one of the
oldest. It draws its water from springs high in the Cairngorms and
its whisky, marketed as a single malt at 70 proof under the name
Old Fettercairn, matures early.

Glen Albyn   Inverness. **H** (65)

In the eighteenth century Inverness was the chief malting town in Scotland and it enjoyed a near monopoly of the trade supplying most of the northern counties and the Hebrides. Glen Albyn was built on the ruins of one of the many breweries in the town in 1846. In 1866 its licence was revoked because of alleged smuggling and it was converted into a flour mill. In 1884 it was re-sited alongside the entrance to Telford's Caledonian canal. Its output is used for blending. Nearby is the company's other distillery, Glen Mhor; although it too draws its water from Loch Ness its whisky has an entirely different taste.

Glenallachie   Aberlour, Banffshire. **H** (66)

Near the Spey and in the shadow of Ben Rinnes, whence it draws its water, the distillery was built in 1967 and like all the postwar Speyside distilleries is white-walled and modestly unassuming, blending as skilfully as it can into its Highland background.

Glenburgie-Glenlivet   Forres, Morayshire. **H** (67)

Four miles from Forres, the distillery was founded in 1810 by the grandfather of the celebrated Victorian surgeon Dr Liston Paul. The water wheel was originally driven by a small burn and the distillery was sited in the middle of some of the finest barley fields in the north. Although it is 20 miles from Glenlivet its owners Hiram Walker feel justified in their hyphenated attachment to that noble area. The product is found in Glencraig vatted malt and the 'Old Smuggler' blend. Glenburgie's production has been continuous since it was founded and it therefore must lay claim to being one of the longest working distilleries in Scotland, if not *the* longest.

Glencadam   Brechin, Angus. **H** (68)

Another subsidiary of Hiram Walker, this distillery was built in 1825 and it derived its water from Moorfoot loch. In the late 1890s its annual output was 40,000 gallons; today it has a capacity of half a million gallons.

Glendeveron   *See* Macduff

Glendronach   Huntly, Aberdeenshire. **H** (69)

The distillery lies about five miles north east of Huntly in the Valley of Forgue. The Dronach burn runs through the works

works which were built in 1826. Barnard recorded that of its six
bonded warehouses one was celebrated for maturing the whisky in
two or three years owing to a peculiarity of the atmosphere
whereas the whisky lying in the others needed five years to attain
the same mellowness. The malt is sold now at 8 and 12 years old.
Although the distillery, owned since 1960 by William Teacher,
has increased its capacity and the still house is ultra modern, it has
kept its old floor maltings.

Glendullan   Dufftown, Banffshire. **H** (70)

Part Victorian, part modern, this was the last of the seven famous
Dufftown distilleries to be built. The distillery, on the A920 going
north east from Dufftown, is owned by the D.C.L. and is
surrounded by thick woods and beech trees. The River Fiddich
runs nearby and supplies all the water needed for cooling purposes
while the water for distilling is collected in two large cisterns two
miles away in the Bogbuie hills.

Glen Elgin   Longmorn, Elgin, Morayshire. **H** (71)

Founded in 1898 by the White Horse man Peter Mackie, the
distillery, one of the last to be built in the boom years at the end of
the 19th century, lies in a beautiful part of Morayshire and you
may well not notice it when confronted with the panoramic views
as you drop down from the Glen of Rhoes to the plain of Moray.
The site was originally chosen partly because it was near
Longmorn station. Its water comes from springs in Glen Rothes
and output was trebled in 1963. Glen Elgin is available as a single
malt.

Glenfarclas-Glenlivet   Ballindalloch, Banffshire. **H** (72)

The distillery, which was built in 1836, stands isolated at the base
of Ben Rinnes where the Avon joins the Spey. There is a fine
museum and a visitor centre which is furnished with panelling
from the liner *Australia*. Although the old maltings were closed in
1972 there is a first class display of the techniques of whisky-
making and a reconstructed whisky bothy. Glenfarclas is still
controlled by the Grant family, which bought it in 1865, and its
malt whisky is outstanding.

Glenfiddich   Dufftown, Banffshire. **H** (73)

In 1886 William Grant invested his entire capital of £775 in the
building of this distillery and the first whisky ran from the stills on
Christmas Day 1887. Glenfiddich is the only Speyside distillery to
do its own bottling and this privately owned firm dominates the

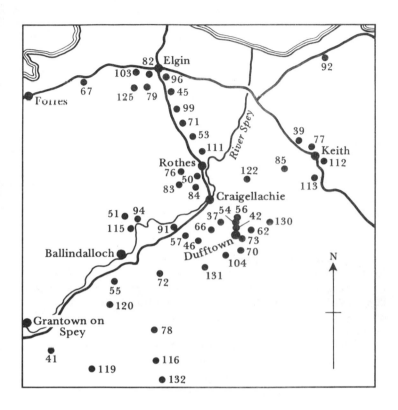

Key to map of Speyside — Highland Malt Distilleries

37 Aberlour-Glenlivet	70 Glendullan	99 Longmorn-Glenlivet
39 Aultmore	71 Glen Elgin	100 Macallan-Glenlivet
41 Balmenach	72 Glenfarclas-Glenlivet	103 Miltonduff-Glenlivet
42 Balvenie	73 Glenfiddich	104 Mortlach
45 Benriach-Glenlivet	76 Glen Grant-Glenlivet	111 Speyburn
46 Benrinnes	77 Glen Keith-Glenlivet	112 Strathisla-Glenlivet
50 Caperdonich	78 Glenlivet, The	113 Strathmill
51 Cardow	79 Glenlossie	115 Tamdhu-Glenlivet
53 Coleburn	82 Glen Moray-Glenlivet	116 Tamnavulin-Glenlivet
54 Convalmore	83 Glenrothes-Glenlivet	119 Tomintoul-Glenlivet
55 Cragganmore	84 Glen Spey	120 Tormore
56 Craigellachie	85 Glentauchers	122 Auchroisk
57 Dailuaine	91 Imperial	125 Mannochmore
62 Dufftown-Glenlivet	92 Inchgower	130 Pittyvaich-Glenlivet
66 Glenallachie	94 Knockando	131 Allta' Bhainne
67 Glenburgie-Glenlivet	96 Linkwood	132 Braes of Glenlivet

world malt export market. The stills are the smallest in Scotland, some fired by gas, some by coal. Much of the output goes into the family blend, originally known as Standfast, the war cry used by the men of Clan Grant at Culloden. This progressive firm converted their original malt barn into a visitor centre in 1969. Each year 50,000 free drams are given away as a striking testimony both to skilled public relations and old world Highland hospitality.

Glen Flagler   *See* Moffat

Glen Foyle   Gargunnock, Stirlingshire. **H** (129)

Glengarioch   Old Meldrum, Aberdeenshire. **H** (127)

Taking its name from the valley of the Garioch, long known as the Granary of Aberdeenshire, and founded in 1797, the distillery is one of the few left malting some of its own barley. In other ways it is looking to the future. In 1977 it was decided to utilise the 12,000 gallons an hour of hot water, which is one of the by-products of whisky-making, and the abundant supplies of local peat in cultivating tomatoes under glass. Not only can the atmosphere be kept at 20°C throughout the year but another by-product, carbon dioxide, is used to boost the normal 300 parts per million of CO_2 in the air to three or four times that amount, thus enabling the plants to grow stronger and faster. Closed in 1968 due to lack of water, the distillery was re-opened after well-boring. Visitors are as welcome here as they are at the company's other distillery, Bowmore. The whisky bottled since 1972 as a single malt also forms a part of the blend Rob Roy.

Glenglassaugh   Portsoy, Banffshire. **H** (74)

The distillery was built in 1875 on the slopes of a steep hill close to the sea from which it is screened by a sandy hill — water comes from the river Glassaugh. Originally an 80-acre farm provided most of the barley needed for the annual production of 80,000 gallons. In 1964 it was almost entirely rebuilt and its output goes for blending in the products of Highland Distilleries.

Glengoyne   Dumgoyne, Stirlingshire. **H** (75)

Sited at the foot of Dumgoyne hill and set in a glen down which pours a picturesque waterfall, the distillery lies in Rob Roy country. Marshal of the R.A.F. Lord Tedder was born close to the distillery where his father was Excise Officer. The reception centre overlooks the waterfall and through the passage of the year the glen is enflowered first with snowdrops, then daffodils which give way in the late Spring to bluebells and finally to the rhododendrons of early summer. The distillery was built in 1833 as Glenguin and bought in 1876 by Lang Bros. It lies on the main Glasgow-Aberfoyle road and although it was modernised in 1966 much of the character remains. The whisky forms the basis for such blends as Red Hackle and Cutty Sark and is also marketed as a single malt at 8 years old and 80 proof. The distillery stands on the Highland line and its whisky is regarded as a Lowland malt for blending purposes.

Glen Grant-Glenlivet   Rothes, Morayshire. **H** (76)

The village of Rothes is not far from the sea and it was near the famous barley-growing plains of Moray. This led to its being selected in 1840 by Major James Grant as the site of what is now one of the most famous single malts in the world. For more than 39 years it was the only distillery in Rothes, until it was joined by Glen Rothes and Glen Spey. It was the first manufactory to have electric light in the north of Scotland. The fame of its whisky is said to be due to the expertise of a former manager of Linkwood distillery called George Grant who took over Glen Grant at the age of 24. Despite controversy about the merits and demerits of each, Glen Grant uses both coal-fired and gas-fired stills. Acquired in 1978 by Seagrams, Glen Grant along with The Glenlivet and Longmorn is one of the three Spey whiskies found in the Queen Anne blend. The original painting of the two Highlanders supporting, or perhaps being supported, by a cask, which forms the Glen Grant label can be seen in the distillery. Many connoisseurs consider Glen Grant to be the most perfect malt made and it is bottled at various proofs and ages.

Glen Grant Distillery (Courtyard)

Glen Keith-Glenlivet   Keith, Banffshire. **H** (77)

Built in 1958 opposite Strathisla-Glenlivet by Chivas Brothers on the site of an old flour and meal mill. The whisky is used for blending.

Glenkinchie   Pencaitland, East Lothian. **L** (3)

Lying in what is known as the Garden of Scotland, the distillery is sited in the Glen of Kinchie, a tributary of the River Tyne, and is beautifully maintained. In the old days its barley was obtained from farming land round the Firth of Forth. The manager, a great enthusiast, recently tracked down a model of a distillery made for the Empire Exhibition at Wembley in 1924. He has refurbished it and, along with a fascinating array of whisky memorabilia, it is now on display. There is, I believe, a French-speaking guide on hand. Glenkinchie's whisky is used entirely for blending.

The Glenlivet   Glenlivet, Banffshire. **H** (78)

I have described elsewhere how George Smith became the first Speyside man to set up a legal distillery (pp 000-000). The distillery stands exposed on a barren hillside and produces a delicate and full-flavoured whisky which is unarguably the most

The Glenlivet Distillery

famous, if not the greatest, in the world. As the old rhyme goes:

> Glenlivet has its castles three
> Drumin, Blairfindy and Deskie
> And also one distillery
> More famous than the castles three.

It has also on at least one occasion been the vehicle of royal preferment. Elizabeth Grant of Rothiemurchus describes how when George IV came to Scotland he demanded his favourite smuggled whisky, Glenlivet, for he drank nothing else: 'My father sent word to me to empty my pet bin where whisky was long in wood, long in uncorked bottles, mild as milk and the true contraband *gout* in it. Much as I grudged this treasure it made our fortunes afterwards, showing on what trifles great events depend. The whisky, and fifty brace of ptarmigan all shot by one man, went up to Holyrood House, and were graciously received and made much of, and a reminder of this attention at a proper moment by the gentlemanly Chamberlain ensured my father the Indian judgeship.'

Glenlochy   Fort William, Inverness-shire. **H** (124)

Not far from Loch Lochy at the Western end of the Caledonian Canal, the distillery was built in 1898; its production goes for blending by Scottish Malt Distillers.

Glenlossie   Elgin, Banffshire. **H** (79)

Three and a half miles south west of Elgin, one of the most elegant of northern towns, the 1876 distillery takes its name from the river Lossie which runs 26 miles to the Moray Firth and flows into the sea at Lossiemouth. A subsidiary of D.C.L., its whisky is used for blending.

Glen Mhor   Inverness. **H** (80)

Founded in 1892 and only a hundred yards or so away from Glen Albyn, it was the first distillery in Scotland to instal mechanical maltings. Named after the Great Glen (*mhor* is the Gaelic for big) it uses water from Loch Ness and it is generally regarded as a big whisky — in David Daiches' words, 'one of the truly great postprandial whiskies, full, rich and mellow.'

Glenmorangie   Tain, Ross-shire. **H** (81)

Overlooking the Dornoch Firth, the distillery has been producing whisky since 1842 and was bought in 1918 by two young men in the whisky trade, Roderick Macdonald and Alexander Muir, who had been using the product in their blends. Glenmorangie still malts its own barley and the whisky which is self-coloured is not matured in sherry casks. The water supply, hard and rich in minerals, comes from the hills of Tarlogie, the peat for malting from Pitsligo in Aberdeenshire. In 1880 Glenmorangie became one of the first distilleries to heat its stills with steam instead of direct firing, thus eliminating the risk of scorching the liquid and affecting the flavour. The company is run by David Macdonald, a third generation member of the family, and there are few finer malts produced in Scotland. The name is pronounced with the accent on the short second syllable: Glen*mor*angie

Glen Moray-Glenlivet   Elgin, Morayshire. **H** (82)

Another distillery also owned by Macdonald & Muir and built in 1897. Its single malt is sold at 10 years old and 70 proof.

Glen Rothes-Glenlivet   Rothes, Morayshire. **H** (83)

One of the great distilling centres of Scotland, Rothes lies on the right bank of the river Spey overlooked by Ben Aigan and Conerock Hill. The distillery was built in 1878 on the banks of the Rothes burn which flows from the Mannock hills, and its first spirit was condensed on the night that the silvery bridge o'er the river Tay was hurled down in a gale, in 1879.

Glen Scotia   Campbeltown, Argyll. **C** (34)

Scotia distillery, as it was originally known, was built in 1832 and its water came from the Crosshill Loch and a couple of 80 foot wells. The malt house still remains but the malt now comes from Kirkcaldy.

Glen Spey   Rothes, Morayshire. **H** (84)

Built in 1885 beneath the hill on which stand the ruins of the Castle of Rothes, former seat of the Earls of Rothes.

Glentauchers   Mulben, Banffshire. (85)

Built in 1898 and owned by James Buchanan, a subsidiary of D.C.L. Its six stills produce whisky for blending purposes only.

Glenturret   Crieff, Perthshire. **H** (86)

The distillery is two miles north west of the town, picturesquely planted on the banks of the river Turret which rises on the slopes of the 3000 feet high Benchonzie. One of the oldest in Scotland, built in 1775, Glenturret closed in the depression of the early twenties and rose as a fully automated phoenix in 1959. In 1974 Glenturret was awarded a Gold Seal at the International Wines and Spirits Competition — perhaps it's all to do with the miniscule size of the stills.

Glenugie Peterhead, Aberdeenshire. **H** (87)

The distillery, which was built in 1875, lies south of Peterhead on the Aberdeen road near the seashore. The owners are Long John International.

Glenury Stonehaven, Kincardineshire. **H** (88)

Established in 1836 by Captain Barclay Allardice, Laird of Ury, the distillery lies to the north of the lovely little port of Stonehaven. Mainly used in blending, the whisky is available at 12 years old and 70 proof.

Highland Park Kirkwall, Orkney. **H** (89)

The distillery site in Kirkwall was where the smuggler Magnus Eunson discharged part of his vocation. By profession he was a preacher and kept a stock of illicit whisky habitually under his pulpit. 'This godly person,' Barnard wrote, 'was accustomed to give out the psalms in a more unctuous manner than usual if the Excise officers were in church.' In the nineteenth century the grain used for malting was the old fashioned 'bere', some of which is still grown in Orkney for the making of beremeal bannocks. It has a very malty taste and the only mill that grinds beremeal these days, water-driven, is in the capable hands of a woman. In the old days faggots of heather were used with the peat in drying the malt, a practice which is, as far as I know, still in use today and which imparted a delicate flavour to the whisky. The original floor maltings are still in use too. The peat comes from the hillside, not as in other parts of the country from low-lying peat mosses — once it was exported to the mainland distilleries. Sited on a hill, the distillery has to pump its water up and that must be unique too. The whisky is available in bottle and is one of the most prized malts made.

Hillside Montrose, Angus. **H** (90)

In 1897 a Dundee whisky merchant called James Isles went into partnership with Septimus Passonage & Co. and established a distillery under the name of Highland Esk. It continued to operate until the outbreak of World War One when it was requisitioned by the army as a barracks. A fire destroyed part of the distillery and it was used purely for malting until 1938 when Associated Scottish Distilleries refurbished the place and opened it as Montrose Distillery. World War Two interrupted distilling once again and when D.C.L. bought the distillery in 1954 they suspended the production of whisky and used only the maltings and the warehouses. Between 1959 and 1964 D.C.L. produced grain whisky at Hillside but the operation was not economic. In 1964 the distillery was extensively reconstructed, the patent still was replaced by pot stills and malt whisky began to flow again in November 1965.

Imperial   Carron, Strathspey. **H** (91)

The distillery was built in 1897 by the owner of Talisker and Dailuaine, one Thomas Mackenzie. In 1899 Imperial was closed and it didn't open again until 1919. Whisky was made until 1925 when distilling was abandoned in favour of maltings. In 1955 the distillery was reconstructed and in the sixties output was doubled and the floor maltings were replaced with five Saladin boxes for mechanical malting.

Inchgower   Buckie, Banffshire. **H** (92)

The distillery lies close to the mouth of the Spey, near the town of Buckie in an area noted for illicit whisky-making and smuggling centred on the famous Bin Hill of Cullen. The original distillery

Inchgower Distillery (Courtyard)

had been established in 1822 at Tochieneal and was removed to Inchgower, in the heart of the barley-growing area, in 1871. It draws its water from the Letter burn which flows through peat mosses, and also from the water of Aultmoor. A clean and mellow malt, it has been available since 1972 at 12 years old and 70 proof. The distillery is owned by Arthur Bell & Sons, who bought it in 1936.

Inverleven   Dumbarton. L (4)

The complex was erected in 1938 and both grain and malt distilling, blending and bottling occur on the one site. A unique way to see almost the whole process of whisky making in one visit. Classed as a Lowland malt the distillery is sited on the mythical Highland line. Visits begin at 10.30 and 2.30.

Jura   Isle of Jura. H (93)

Jura is 28 miles long and eight miles wide and it has a population of only 180 — it has one distillery, one hotel and no police force. The distillery is tucked into the hillside opposite Craighouse Hotel. The Campbells of Jura built it in the middle of the nineteenth century and whisky was distilled until the turn of the century when the bottom fell out of the market. To avoid tax the building was unroofed and the buildings became derelict. In 1958 a new distillery was put on the drawing board and it started production in 1963. The water comes from a thousand feet up in the hills and passes through a cave which was once a haunt of smugglers. The first bottling of Isle of Jura malt matured in bond on the island was in 1974. George Orwell wrote *Animal Farm* in a farmhouse called Barnhill at the north end of the island.

Kinclaith   Ballater Street, Glasgow. L (5)

Built in 1957 by Long John Distillers Ltd., its water comes from Loch Katrine.

Knockando   Morayshire. H (94)

On the scenic route down the Speyside, Knockando was built in 1898 and is controlled by I.D.V.

Knockdhu   Knock, Banffshire. H (95)

A historically interesting distillery this, certainly for the economist. In the 1880s the Scottish malt distillers became increasingly dismayed by the inroads that cheap blended whisky (high proportions of patent still whisky and small amounts of the more expensive malt) was making not only on their business interests but on the good name of whisky itself. It looked as if they might well petition the government to enforce the Act of Parliament which prevented retailers from selling goods which were 'not of the nature, substance and quality demanded.' Blenders, fearful of losing their supplies of malt whisky, began protecting their sources of supply, either by buying distilleries or building them — between 1880 and the end of the century 30 distilleries were bought and many more passed into the hands of the Edinburgh and Glasgow whisky entrepreneurs. It was for these reasons that D.C.L., with their massive grain-oriented base, built in 1893 their first malt distillery — Knockdhu. Today, as we have seen, they control 43.

Ladyburn   Girvan, Ayrshire. **L** (6)

The Girvan complex was opened by Grant's (of Glenfiddich and Balvenie fame) in 1963. It makes gin, vodka, grain whisky and a malt. Visitors are welcomed.

Lagavulin   Port Ellen, Islay. **I** (17)

Lagavulin ('the mill in the valley') is thought to have been the scene of illicit distillation as early as the 1740s. 'As we rounded a ridge,' wrote Barnard, 'we came in sight of the historical ruin of Dun-naomhaig Castle which stands on a large peninsular rock, protected on the land side by a thick earthen mound opposite the village of Lagavulin'. Here Robert Bruce took refuge after his defeat by the Earl of Pembroke and it was a stronghold for the

Lagavulin Distillery

Lords of the Isles. The early 'moonlight' whisky was made in little bothies and right up to 1821 smuggling was a popular hobby in Islay. Early in the century the buildings were converted into a legal distillery and in 1835 they were bought by J.L. Mackie & Co., who were eventually to produce White Horse. In 1908 the adjoining distillery Malt Mill was built and floor malting continued until 1973. The malt is highly delightful and is marketed at 12 years old and 75 proof.

Laphroaig   Port Ellen, Islay. **I** (18)

The distillery is a mile away from Port Ellen and is built right down on the seashore; on a stormy day the spray will lather your face as you enter the buildings. Founded in 1820, Laphroaig still malts its own barley and although you can see Ireland on a fine day from the manager's office the whisky owes nothing to Ireland; it is heavily peated and once drunk never forgotten. The distillery is owned by Long John but until recently the head of the company was Mrs Wishart Campbell, the only woman distiller in Scotland. If you find Laphroaig too powerful you can enjoy it in more muted form in Islay Mist — an 8 year old blended whisky which many people confuse with a vatted malt. It contains (besides Laphroaig), Smith's Glenlivet and Glen Grant. As for the unique smell and flavour of Laphroaig there are those who say it reminds them of seaweed and iodine, others have likened it to cough mixture. Too dominating for casual drinking (as lief approach Wagner casually) it makes an excellent after-dinner dram. On a cold winter's day, drunk from the decanter at noon in the distillery, it takes a lot of beating.

Ledaig   *See* Tobermory, Isle of Mull.

Linkwood   Elgin, Morayshire. **H** (96)

One mile south east of Elgin, the distillery was built in 1821 by William Brown and it is said that so strict was the regime of its most famous manager, Roderick Mackenzie, that nothing was replaced or moved until it was absolutely necessary; even spiders' webs were allowed to remain in case their departure should in some mystical way affect the brew. Linkwood, rebuilt and re-equipped in 1963, produces a light malt with a pleasant flavour bottled at 12 years old and 75 proof.

Linlithgow   *See* St. Magdalene.

Littlemill   Bowling, Dunbartonshire. L (7)

Close to the Clyde and the railway station, Littlemill is 12 miles from Glasgow and was built about the year 1800. It once used peat both from the Isle of Lewis and from Perthshire and exported its whisky all over the world. Its water comes from the Kilpatrick Hills.

Loch Lomond   Alexandria, Dunbartonshire. H (97)

Built in 1966 and owned by Barton Distilling Ltd. Sited on the Highland line it has its allegiance north of that line not south and its whiskies are found in House of Stuart and Highland Mist.

Lochnagar   Balmoral, Aberdeenshire. H (108)

The first lease of the distillery which is named after the nearby mountain is dated 1824. Queen Victoria and Prince Albert visited the works in 1848 and sampled a dram. John Begg, the founder of the distillery, has left this respectful account of the Royal Descent: 'I observed Her Majesty and the Prince Consort approaching. I ran and opened the door, when the Prince said, "We have come to see through your works, Mr Begg." I endeavoured to explain the whole process of malting, brewing and distilling, showing the Royal Party the barley in its original state and in all its different stages of manufacture until it came out at the mouth of the still pipe in spirits. When we came to the door I asked H.R.H. if he would like to taste the spirit in its matured state. H.R.H. having agreed to do this, I called for a bottle and glasses and presenting one glass to Her Majesty, she tasted it. So also did his Royal Highness the Prince. I then presented a glass to the Princess Royal and to the Prince of Wales and Prince Alfred all of whom tasted the spirit. H.R.H. the Prince of Wales was going to carry his glass quickly to his mouth. I checked him saying it was very strong and so he did not take but a very small drop. John Begg at full distillery strength may be taken only in small pegs — even by Royalty!' Thereafter, Lucky Begg's distillery, and his whisky, was known as Royal Lochnagar. A few years ago, for reasons which they decline to reveal, D.C.L., the present owners, decided to dispense with history and drop the royal prefix.

Lochside   Montrose, Angus. H (98)

Built in 1957, the distillery passed into the control of a Madrid firm in 1973. It is equipped both for malt and grain distilling.

Longmorn-Glenlivet   Longmorn, Elgin, Morayshire. (99)

Built in 1894 on the site of a grain mill which had been working since the beginning of the seventeenth century. The peat comes from Mannoch Hill and the water from a spring which has never, fortunately, been known to dry up. I am impressed with Dr R.J.S. MacDowall's suggestion that Longmorn mixed judiciously with Clynelish, The Glenlivet and Macallan's 'makes what is probably the best possible drink in the world.' Longmorn is bottled at 12 years and 70 proof.

Lomond   Montrose. **L** (8)

Owned by Hiram Walker; the stills are straight-sided.

Macallan   Craigellachie, Morayshire. **H** (100)

A great Speyside malt, produced in a distillery which was one of the first to take out a licence in 1824. The company is still run by the family of Roderick Kemp who bought it in 1892. He was a former manager and owner of Talisker and Macallan's is every bit as individual as the Skye malt. The stills are among the smallest in Scotland, not because there is any particular virtue in that but because the door of the coppersmith's room wasn't all that big and he made them just the right size to pass through. For a period during this century Macallan added the 'Glenlivet' to its name but this has now been dropped. Bottled at 10 and 15 years old, it is a whisky which needs no exterior support.

Macduff   Banff. **H** (101)

Built in 1966, the distillery produces a single malt which is marketed under the name Glendeveron, after the river Deveron from which the condensing water is taken. It is bottled at 8 years old and 70 proof.

Mannochmore   Birnie, Morayshire. **H** (12)

Opened in 1972, this new D.C.L. distillery adjoins the company's existing Glenlossie Distillery but draws its water from a different source. Output is about a million proof gallons a year. Also on the site is a new by-product recovery plant which not only purifies the effluent before it is discharged into the river but processes draff and a syrup obtained from evaporating pot ale to produce a high-protein feed for cattle, sheep and poultry known as Distillers Dark Grains.

Millburn   Inverness. **H** (102)

The distillery, near the junction of the Aberdeen and Perth roads about a mile from the centre of the town, was established in 1807 and almost entirely rebuilt in 1876. It took its name from the Mill Burn. The floor maltings were closed in 1964 and replaced by mechanical maltings.

Milton   *See* Strathisla-Glenlivet.

Miltonduff-Glenlivet   Elgin. **H** (103)

Built in 1824 on the site of earlier and illegal activities, Miltonduff at one time used the technique of triple distillation. Pluscarden, where the distillery is sited, was once a Benedictine stronghold and the old mash house is thought to have been built on the site of the priory brewhouse. Water comes from the Black Hills. The malt is bottled at 12 years old and 75 proof.

Miltonduff Distillery

Moffat   Airdrie, Lanarkshire. **L** (11)

A former paper mill which was converted in 1964 into a grain and malt distillery by Inverhouse Distillers, an American company. Its malt whisky, Glen Flagler, is by far the cheapest on the market and is highly popular in cut-price liquor marts.

Mortlach   Dufftown. **H** (104)

Mortlach church and churchyard are famous as the scene in the year 1010 of the victory by Malcolm II over a small army of Danes. The distillery was built in 1823 and rebuilt and re-equipped in 1903. It produces a lightly peated malt which is bottled at 12 years old and 70 proof.

North Port   Brechin, Forfar. **H** (105)

Lying half a mile from the River South Esk, the distillery was built in 1820 and its water was brought from the Grampians by pipeline. Originally the spirit was condensed in worms laid in the bed of the Den Burn which ran through the distillery grounds.

Oban   Argyll. **H** (126)

Oban is the great jumping-off ground for Mull, Iona, the curious isle of Staffa and the Outer Hebridean islands and its distillery was built in 1794 by the Stevenson family, who converted Oban from a tiny fishing village into a tiny town. The company which owned the distillery suffered a severe blow with the collapse of the notorious brothers, Robert and Walter Pattison. They began with a grocery business in Leith; climbing aboard the blended whisky train as it gathered speed, they acquired wealth, distilleries and far too much credit from the banks. At the end of last century everyone wanted to 'be in whisky', it was the big growth market. The crash came in 1898, brought on by an excess of production over demand, a fevered period of gambling and speculation by investors and then a gradual realisation that the Pattisons were not as adept at managing money as they were at getting and spending it. The two brothers appeared before the Criminal Court and were sentenced to eighteen and eight months imprisonment respectively. Oban which had sold all its output to the Pattisons suffered an almost mortal blow along with many other distilleries. It was a direct result of the collapse of Pattisons that D.C.L. was able to speed up its policy of amalgamation by acquiring large stocks of whisky and real estate at knockdown prices. Oban is now owned by D.C.L.

Ord   Muir of Ord, Inverness-shire. **H** (106)

The first licence was taken out in 1838 by a Mr McLennan who may or may not, in the manner of the times, have been a freelance distiller; certainly the site was well known to local people, if not to the gaugers, as a source of good whisky. In 1961 the old floor maltings were replaced by six Saladin boxes for mechanical malting and in 1968 18 drum maltings were installed. The whisky goes entirely for blending.

Pittyvaich-Glenlivet   Dufftown, Morayshire. **H** (130)

When Bell's bought Dufftown-Glenlivet distillery in 1933 they also acquired the extensive lands of Pittyvaich Farm, Pittyvaich Woodlands and Pittyvaich Shootings. In 1973 they erected an ultra-modern distillery on part of this high-lying land. Its manager is not a whisky-maker but an engineer. A sign of the times?

Port Ellen   Islay. I (19)

The distillery is planted on the seashore and was opened in 1825. It also houses a large D.C.L. maltings which provides malt for the company's distilleries on the island: Port Ellen itself, Caol Ila, and Lagavulin. The distillery closed down in 1930 and was not reopened until 1965.

Pulteney   Wick, Caithness. H (107)

The town of Wick is divided by a river and the south side where the distillery is located is known as Pulteney Town. It is the most northerly mainland distillery and was built in 1826. Closed during the slump after the First World War, it wasn't re-opened until 1951. In the 1960s the stills were increased in size. Neil Gunn, a native of Wick, recalls seeing Pulteney malt as a child. It was perfectly clear and certainly new: 'In those days it was potent stuff, consumed, I should say on the quays of Wick more for its effect than its flavour! Though very pronounced in flavour, it was never quite so peaty as some of the Speyside stills which occasionally err just a trifle in that respect I think.' Try it yourself: it's bottled at 8 years old and 70 proof.

Pulteney Distillery

Rosebank   Falkirk. L (9)

Built in 1842 on the banks of the old Forth and Clyde canal a mile from Falkirk, the distillery was one of the many in the Lowlands which ran into serious financial difficulties when the whisky bubble burst at the beginning of this century. There is a reception centre but neither banks nor roses; the very potable malt is bottled at 8 years old and 70 proof.

Royal Brackla   Nairn, Morayshire. **H** (108)

The distillery was founded in 1812 by Captain William Fraser who purveyed his whisky to King William IV and acquired both a regal prefix and a Royal Warrant in 1835. The *Morning Chronicle* of 20th January that year contained this puff: 'BRACKLA or THE KING'S WHISKY — His Majesty having been pleased to distinguish this "by His Royal Command to supply his establishment" has placed this whisky first on the List of British Spirits, and when known should in truth be termed "The Drink Divine".' Like many other licit distillers in the pre-1823 period Fraser found business far from easy. Giving evidence to the Parliamentary Commission which was appointed to look into the activities of the smugglers he claimed that he had 'not sold 100 gallons for consumption within 120 miles of his residence during the past year, though people drank nothing but whisky.' At that time legally distilled malt whisky sold at 9s 6d a gallon and was relatively weak — only 7 degrees over proof. Smuggled whisky with its heady flavour of illegality was to be had at 20 degrees over proof for as little as 6s a gallon.

Royal Lochnagar   *See* Lochnagar

St Magdalene   Linlithgow, West Lothian. **L** (10)

At one time there were five distilleries in the royal burgh of Linlithgow, birthplace of Mary Queen of Scots and former seat of royalty. St Magdalene, or Linlithgow as D.C.L. now prefers to call it, dates from the eighteenth century and takes its name from the lands of St Magdalene's Cross which the original owner feu'd from the Countess of Dalhousie. Just before World War One intense competition among the Lowland distilleries forced the company which owned St Magdalene to go into liquidation and D.C.L. gained control. Thereafter, D.C.L. tells me, they 'opened negotiations with the other Lowland malt distillers with a view to the elimination or limitation of this competition. As a result, five malt distilleries were brought together by the incorporation of Scottish malt Distillers in 1914.'

Scapa   Kirkwall, Orkney. **H** (110)

Opened in October 1885, Scapa has none of the fame of Highland

Park. It lies on the banks of the Lingro burn at the head of Scapa
Bay, one time haven for the Royal Navy battle fleet, now busy
with oil activity. A few yards from the distillery are the remains of
a Pictish broch. The distillery is owned by Hiram Walker of
Ontario.

Speyburn   Rothes, Morayshire. **H** (111)

The distillery occupies a very attractive site just off the main
Elgin-Rothes road outside the town. When it was built in 1897
there was a keen determination to finish the stillhouse by the end
of the year so that the first fillings could legitimately claim to have
been produced in the Diamond Jubilee Year of Queen Victoria,
Empress of India. In December the first mash was made and the
stills were fired — one butt was bonded bearing the magic 1897
date. Speyburn was a conservation pioneer; in the early years of
this century the company joined with other nearby distillers and
built an evaporating and drying plant to recycle pot ale. The
plant produced a low-grade fertiliser called 'Maltassa'.

Speyside   Kingussie. **H** (128)

This is a revival of the old Speyside distillery which was operating
at the turn of the century. New stills were installed in 1972.

Springbank   Campbeltown. **C** (25)

Springbank in the centre of Campbeltown, the Whisky City, has
been in the hands of the Mitchell family since it was established in
1828. A highly regarded malt, it is bottled on the premises at 80
proof and 12 years old. The distillery is still using its old floor
maltings and it redistills its foreshots and feints in a second still
instead of returning them to the feints receiver to be reworked in
the low wines still — a similar process to the one used in
Auchentoshan.

Strathisla-Glenlivet   Keith, Banffshire. **H** (112)

The distillery is bounded by the river Isla which rises at Loch
Park, Drummuir, seven miles away. It falls over a small cascade
just before it reaches the distillery, which was established in 1786,
making it one of the eight oldest in Scotland. The water used in
distilling came from the Broomhill Spring; it was collected in a
reservoir and then mixed with a small quantity of water from the
Isla and the make of whisky produced was marketed as 'Strathisla'
although the distillery itself was always known as Milton. When
Seagrams bought Milton in 1950 they changed its name to
Strathisla-Glenlivet and added a picturesque water wheel to the

old buildings. Its whisky is to be found both in Chivas Regal and 100 Pipers and it is bottled as a single malt at 8 and 15 years old.

Strathmill   Keith, Banffshire. **H** (113)

In 1892 an old 1823 flour mill was converted into a distillery. It was bought by the Gilbey brothers in 1895 and is now owned by I.D.V. The whisky goes entirely for blending.

Talisker   Carbost, Isle of Skye. **H** (114)

One of the most beautifully placed distilleries of all, Talisker lies on the shores of Loch Harport in the small hamlet of Carbost. It was set up by Hugh and Kenneth MacAskill of Talisker House, sheep farmers who were granted a lease by MacLeod of MacLeod, in 1830. A local preacher denounced it as 'one of the greatest curses that in the ordinary course of Providence, could befall this or any other place.' Talisker has had a moveable career. Originally sited at Snizort it closed in mysterious circumstances and the stills were then transported to Fiscavaig but Providence intervened again; the supply of water proved inadequate, so finally the apparatus was moved to Carbost. Here it worked happily until 1960 when a disastrous fire in the stillhouse put it out of action for two years. Now almost completely rebuilt, the distillery takes its malt from the mainland but the whisky's highly unique and powerful flavour is unchanged. It is rumoured to be former Prime Minister Edward Heath's favourite malt and was eulogised by Robert Louis Stevenson:

> The King o' drinks, as I conceive it,
> Talisker, Isla or Glenlivet.

It is bottled at various ages and strengths.

Tamdhu-Glenlivet   Knockando, Banffshire. **H** (115)

Built in 1897 on the banks of the Spey and owned by Highland Distilleries. The malt is bottled at 8 years old and 70 proof. There is a reception centre.

Tamnavulin-Glenlivet   Ballindalloch, Banffshire. **H** (116)

The distillery stands on the west bank of the River Spey at Ballindalloch and takes its name from an old water mill (Tamnavulin is the Gaelic for 'the mill on the hill'). It was built in the 1960s and like all postwar distilleries is engineered to be operated by a handful of technicians. Owned by Invergordon Distillers, it is to be·found among other blends in Glenfoyle Reserve and is also bottled as 75 proof 8-year-old single malt.

Teaninich   Alness, Ross-shire. **H** (117)

The distillery lies on the margin of the sea and was built in 1800. When Barnard visited it in the 1890s he was as impressed as we might be today by one of the new automated Speyside distilleries: 'It is the only Distillery north of Inverness that is lighted by electricity; besides which it possesses telephonic communication with the Proprietor's residence and the quarters of the Excise Officers!'

Tobermory   Isle of Mull. **H** (123)

The distillery was built in 1823 at the southern end of the village in the form of a triangle; it is overshadowed by a high cliff down which falls from its source in the Mishnish Lochs the cascading waters of the Tobermory river. It was closed in 1924 as an uneconomic proposition. In 1972 a private consortium invested £350,000, added two new stills, gave employment to nine people and began distilling for a target of 600,000 gallons a year. The venture was shortlived; the enterprise was placed in the hands of the receiver. In June 1978 there was good news for the picturesque little town of Tobermory, in whose bay lie the sunken remains of an Armada galleon: a West Yorkshire businessman from Cleckheaton had raised enough money to start distilling once again. Fingers are being kept firmly crossed and questions hang in the air. Who will want to lay down fillings of an unproved whisky? Where will the money come from to provide an investment on which, by law, there can be no return for at least three years? In the old days the whisky made at the distillery was known as Old Mull; perhaps the new owner's decision to rename the distillery Tobermory (intervening owners had called it Ledaig) may have a magical effect on its viability.

Tobermory Distillery

Tomatin   Tomatin, Inverness-shire. **H** (118)

The distillery, built in 1897, is surrounded by moorland, once a royal hunting ground attached to the Castle of Inverness which lies 12 miles north up the A9. Tomatin has the distinction of producing more malt whisky than any other distillery in Scotland and its battery of stills work round the clock. Recently the owners spent £100,000 on an imaginative plan to farm eels. Using the vast quantities of warm water produced by the distilling process they are raising elvers in tanks; in 8 months they grow to a length of four feet, a development which would take anything up to two years in unheated water. Tomatin is one of the distilleries which exports its whisky to Japan in bulk. It is also found in the Big T blend and is bottled as a modest single malt.

Tomintoul-Glenlivet   Ballindalloch, Banffshire. (119)

The highest distillery in Scotland, its water comes from the spring of Ballantruan and production began in 1965. In 1974 the whisky was launched in what looks like a large scent bottle as a single malt.

Tormore   Advie, Grantown-on-Spey, Morayshire. (120)

The distillery seven miles north of Grantown-on-Spey, was the first to be built on Speyside since the beginning of the century. The architect, Sir Albert Richardson, created a pleasant complex crowned above the cooperage by a chiming clock and the distillery came 'on-stream' in October 1959. When the distillery was opened in 1960 by the Countess of Seafield a 'time capsule' made in the shape of a pot still was buried in the forecourt. It contained a recording of the chimes, a Tregnum (three bottles) of Long John whisky, a treatise on how Scotch is made, a history of the industry, names of plant employees, an American dollar ('dramatising the importance of the United States market'), the names of all the Scottish clans and samples of the grain, water, peat and cask staves used in the distillery. Interesting artefacts for future archeologists from outer space. The whisky can be bought as a 10-year-old single malt.

Tullibardine   Blackford, Perthshire. (121)

In his epic work Barnard paid tribute to the 'fine character' of the wells of Blackford which produced an excellent beer. Water from these wells was used to brew the ale provided for the coronation of James IV at Scone in 1488. The distillery was opened in 1949 on the site of one of the old Blackford breweries and its excellent light malt is bottled at 10 years and 70 proof and can also be found in Findlater's vatted malt Mar Lodge and their 'Finest' blend.

Grain Distilleries

There are 14 grain distilleries producing between them around 75 million gallons of whisky a year. Most of them, but not all, are to be found in the Lowland towns.

Ben Nevis Fort William
A patent still was added to the original 1825 malt distillery in 1878.

Caledonian Edinburgh
This distillery was built in 1855 near Haymarket station and at one time was the second largest distillery in Britain.

Cambus
Built in 1806 as a malt distillery; a patent still was added in 1830.

Cameronbridge Buckhaven
Built in 1824 by John Haig. A Stein still was added in 1828 and this was superseded by a Coffey Still in 1832. It has the distinction of marketing the only grain whisky in Scotland — Choice Old Cameron Brig.

Carsebridge Alloa
Built at the end of the eighteenth century as a malt distillery it moved to grain distilling with the invention of the Coffey Still.

Dumbarton
Built on the site of an old shipyard by Hiram Walker & Sons in 1937.

Girvan
William Grant & Sons' grain distillery, built on the same site as their Ladyburn malt distillery.

Invergordon
The most northerly grain distillery in Britain; it produced its first whisky in 1961 and is owned by the Invergordon Distillers Group.

Lochside Montrose
Built in 1957.

Moffat Airdrie
Built in 1964 by Inverhouse Distillers.

North British Edinburgh
Established in 1885. See page 27.

Pronunciation Guide

A number of distilleries derive their name from Gaelic which may confuse the non-Scot. The uvular fricative (the *ch* in *loch*) is even more important in Scotland than it is in Germany and this 'och' sound where it occurs should be given its full guttural entitlement. The accented syllables are in italics.

Allta' Bhainne	Alter*vane*
Auchentoshan	*Och*'n'tosh'n
Balmenach	Bal*may*nach
Balvenie	Bal*vee*ny
Bruichladdich	Brewich*laddi*e
Bunnahabhain	Bunner*harv*'n
Caol Ila	C'll *Ee*ler
Clynelish	Clyne*leash*
Dailuaine	Dell*you*in
Dallas Dhu	Dulles *Doo*
Dalwhinnie	Dull*hwinny*
Glenglassaugh	Glen*glass*och
Glenmorangie	Glen*morr*engy
Glenugie	Gl'n*oog*ie
Islay	*Eye*ler
Lagavulin	Lugger*voo*lin
Laphroaig	L'*froig*
Strathisla	Strath*eye*ler
Tomatin	To*mart*'n
Tomintoul	Tom'n*towel*

The Taste of Scotland

Being a northerly land, Scotland has to contend with a shorter growing season than the south; there are hundreds of square miles of breathtakingly beautiful hills and mountains suitable only for the grazing of deer or hardy sheep. At its best, Scottish food is based on raw materials which, like whisky, have no equal elsewhere. Salmon from the Tay and Spey, grouse from the Perthshire moors, venison from the deer forests of the Highlands, Aberdeen Angus beef, mutton from the hills, mountain hare, ptarmigan, capercailzie, wild duck, pheasant — it's a table rich in protein but frequently short of vegetables. Although improvidence is rapidly emptying Scottish waters, try (if you can) a herring grilled in oatmeal, a poached mackerel, creamed Finnan haddie or the giant prawns, crabs, scallops and lobsters which are exported to the five-star restaurants of Europe.

When the Scots are not cooking out of packets and tins — for they take keenly to convenience foods — they can produce a variety of dishes which are both traditional and in many cases historic. For 400 years the Norsemen dominated the islands and coastline of the north and they left behind their skills in preserving and curing fish. The Auld Alliance with France brought a pride in pastry and sweetmeats: haggis and stovies have their roots in France and the housewife in Scotland still orders a 'gigot' at the butcher's, not a leg of lamb.

The Celtic tradition of cooking over open peat fires and baking on a girdle or griddle has led to long-simmered soups and broths and mountains of scones, biscuits, bannocks (oatcakes), buns and pancakes. The tooth is sweet in Scotland and the incidence of dentures is above the average. Helpings tend to be larger than in the south; there is no faddy distaste for carbohydrates; the wind can be cold on the hill — the food is filling.

There is no tradition at all of using whisky in the kitchen — except of course to cheer up the cook. Whisky was distilled for pouring down the throat, not for putting in pots. So don't look for a genuine Scottish equivalent of *boeuf à la bourguignonne, coq au vin*, or *haricots au vin rouge*. What you can look for in Scotland today is a new awareness and pride in traditional dishes and an inventiveness that may well surface in a chocolate whisky gateau or steak Balmoral — tournedos flamed with whisky. But don't confuse Rob Roy's whisky omelette or Flora Macdonald's whisky trifle with food born out of necessity and want.

In 1973 the Scottish Tourist Board launched a campaign to promote dishes that were either traditional or used Scottish produce creatively. They called it 'A Taste of Scotland' and over 300 hotels and restaurants are now providing Scottish fare. These establishments can be identified by the 'Stockpot' sign outside and a free guide to their whereabouts can be obtained from the Board headquarters at 23 Ravelston Terrace, Edinburgh EH4 3EU.

Breakfast

Nowhere in the world will you get a better breakfast than in Scotland, where the tradition of starting the day with a substantial meal goes well back into the eighteenth century. As Dr Johnson wrote without reservation: 'In the breakfast the Scots must be confessed to excel... if an epicure could move by a wish in quest of sensual gratification, wherever he had supped, he would breakfast in Scotland.'

It was the Scots who gave both *brochan* and marmalade to the world. Brochan or porridge is made from oatmeal and boiling water and although consumed by the English as a pudding (they pour sugar on it!) is taken by Scots as a salted dish. The proper way to prepare porridge is to take coarsely ground oatmeal and let it fall into a saucepan of boiling water. After ten minutes of stirring and boiling, add a sufficient quantity of salt and then let it continue to cook for at least half an hour. (In my aunt's house the porridge was left on the fireside all night. Before retiring to bed she filled an appropriate number of bowls with milk; these were left to lie in a cold place all night so that when we came down in the morning the cream had risen to the top and the porridge was so thick you could have cut chunks with a knife. At table we each had a plate of porridge and a bowl of the creamy milk and the right and proper way to eat it was to take a spoonful of porridge and then dip it into the milk to cool before taking it into the mouth.)

After the porridge there may be some kind of smoked, dried or salted fish on the menu. *Arbroath smokies* are whole gutted haddock, hot smoked to a light golden colour. They can be eaten as they are or heated with a little butter. *Finnan Haddock* is split, brined and cold smoked until golden; it's usually poached in water or sometimes milk before being brought to the table. A delicious breakfast treat eaten with brown bread and butter. *Kippers* are split herring, brined and cold smoked over oak shavings. A great delicacy, these — alas, over-fishing has promoted the herring into the luxury class and you may not be lucky enough to find any on the menu. Loch Fyne kippers are generally thought to be the best but they are rivalled by those from Mallaig, Stornoway and Aberdeen.

Bacon and eggs are the great staple of the Scottish breakfast and the bacon will most probably be *Ayrshire*. The cure uses a small side of pork and the boned meat is brined in a pickle which contains brown sugar. The bacon is rolled and left to dry. Grilled, fried or boiled in a piece, it is, to my taste, the best bacon in the world.

End your meal with baps, breakfast rolls or toast and that most Scottish of preserves, marmalade — devised in the eighteenth century by Janet Keiller in Dundee. Don't believe the story about Mary Queen of Scots bringing marmalade from France; it owes its origin to native frugality. James Keiller brought a load of Seville oranges from a Spanish skipper whose ship was stormbound in the port of Dundee. Too bitter to sell, it was the canny Janet who converted them into marmalade.

It takes a Celt to make proper tea, mahogany in colour and so hot it could scald the roof of your mouth, and you may well find that tea is a better breakfast beverage in Scottish hotels than coffee.

Soups and Broths

The pot simmering over the fire filled with anything to hand is also a centuries-old Celtic tradition and a good broth or *bree* as it's sometimes called is usually presented at both lunch and dinner.

Cock-a-leekie is a cock or fowl simmered with sliced-up leeks, to which prunes are sometimes added as sweetening. *Cullen Skink* comes from the fishing village of Cullen on the shores of the Moray Firth. It's a kind of Scottish bouillabaisse, made with Finnan Haddock, potatoes, onions and milk. (Skink is an old Scots term for broth.)

Partan Bree is a rich, creamy crab soup and *Bawd Bree* is broth made from the meat of a hare. *Lorraine Soup* is said to have been brought to Holyrood Palace by Mary of Lorraine, mother of Mary Queen of Scots. It is a rich cream soup made with chicken and flavoured with almonds, lemon and nutmet. *Powsowdie* is sheep's head broth made with carrots, barley, turnips, onions, celery and dried peas. *Barley Kail* contains a piece of shin of beef, the leaves of kail (kale), and barley. But perhaps the most perfect soup of all is just simply called *Scotch Broth*. It can be made with either beef or mutton to which is added a selection of vegetables depending on what is available: cabbage certainly should be there and if possible leek, onion, celery, potato, turnip, carrot and barley. Garnished with parsley, it is almost a meal in itself.

Meat

Scottish beef is available all the year round but is most abundant from July to November: the best known breeds are Aberdeen Angus and Galloway. *Scottish lamb* is available from March to December but is at its best from August to October. The Blackface one-year-old hogget is available from January to March and is at its peak in January and February. Roast or boiled, the meat of Scotland tends to be overdone rather than underdone and those liking their lamb pink and their beef rare may now and again be disappointed.

Some favourite meat dishes which appear on the Scottish table are:

Forfar Bridies Chopped steak with suet in a pastry case.

Potted Hough Minced shin of beef made into a brawn.

Minced Collops A Scottish word derived from escalope. Usually minced beef, although venison, hare and veal may be used.

Gigot of Mutton A leg of mutton boiled with carrots and turnips and served with caper sauce.

Haggis As Scottish as whisky, kilts and bagpipes, the haggis is traditionally eaten at suppers organised to commemorate Scotland's great poet, Robert Burns, and her patron saint, St. Andrew. Burns hailed the haggis as 'Great Chieftain o' the puddin' race.' It is eaten with neeps (turnips) and washed down with copious drams of whisky. Made from the pluck (hearts, lights and liver) of a sheep mixed with suet, toasted oatmeal and seasoning, the whole tasty collation is stuffed into a sheep's paunch and boiled for a considerable time. Haggis is not such an acquired taste as you may be led to believe; many hotels these days serve a small portion as a starter. It is savoury, peppery and as delicate as kedgeree.

Scotch Eggs A hard-boiled egg covered with sausage meat and breadcrumbs and fried in deep fat.

Howtowdie (perhaps from Old French *hutaudeau*) A plump young chicken cooked in a casserole with onions, potatoes and butter.

Venison The meat of the Highland Red Deer or the Roe Deer is yet another delicacy which can be presented roasted, as pasties, minced in collops (escalopes), casseroled, made into a broth or served as chops. Roast haunch of venison, in these days of deep-freeze, is offered by many hotels all the year round.

Roast Bubbly-Jock Turkey, stuffed with a chestnut forcemeat.

Tattie Pot Mutton and potato pie.

Game in Season

The *Red Deer* Stag, at its best in early autumn, can be stalked from 1st July-20th October; the hind, which has less fat and consequently less flavour than the stag, indeed a smaller animal altogether, is in season from 21st October-15th February. The *fallow* and *roe* deer also have their closed seasons.

Capercailzie, also known as the Wood Grouse, and the largest member of the grouse family, has a dark flesh when cooked, braised or stewed and can only be shot between 1st October and 21st January.

Red Grouse The season begins on 12th August and there is a great rush to bring the first grouse of the season down to the London hotels. The young birds are usually roasted, the older casseroled; shooting must cease on December 10th.

Wood Pigeon No close season; at its best between October and May.

Mallard, Teal, Widgeon, three varieties of wild duck, can be taken below the high tide mark from September 1st-February 20th and elsewhere from September 1st-January 31st. Similar shooting restrictions cover the greylag and pinkfoot wild geese.

Other varieties of game bird include the *common snipe, woodcock, partridge, pheasant* and *ptarmigan*.

Vegetables

The Scots are very fond of *potatoes* and the finest are said to come from Ayrshire. There are three 'seasons'. The *early* varieties can be dug from May to July, the *second*, such as Craig's Royal and Great Scot, are ready between August and mid-September and the *main crop* (which includes Redskin, Kerr's Pinks, Golden Wonder, King Edward and Arran Banner) are ready for the winter.

Kale (Kail), Leeks, Sprouts, Carrots, Broccoli, Turnips and *Tomatoes* are found in season and have given rise to several traditional dishes:

Stovies The name is derived from the French *étouffer*, to simmer in a closed pot. Potatoes are simmered with onions in butter or dripping and served with cold meat.

Clapshot An Orkney dish of boiled potatoes and turnips, an ideal accompaniment to haggis.

Rumbledethumps Boiled cabbage and mashed potatoes mixed with butter and chopped chives or onions. Sometimes put in a pie dish, covered with grated cheese and browned under the grill.

Skirlie Oatmeal, onions and suet, fried together and eaten with meat.

Chappit Tatties Mashed boiled potatoes beaten with milk and butter.

Mealie Potatoes Boiled potatoes tossed hot in butter and oatmeal.
Colcannon Cold cabbage and potato, fried with butter or the fat from a joint.
Kailkenny Boiled cabbage and potatoes, mixed with cream.
Bashed Neeps Boiled swede mashed with butter, nutmeg, salt and pepper.

Fish

The two most noted fish in Scotland are the *herring* and the *salmon*. For decades in the Hebrides the staple diet was herring, oatmeal and potatoes; periodically the shoals would for mysterious reasons disappear and then a period of hardship and want ensued. Today the herring has been fished almost to extinction, so perhaps you will not see it on your plate — more's the pity; grilled in oatmeal it was every bit as good as salmon.

The salmon fortunately still runs, returning each year from the deep sea to spawn in the river of its origin; it is a spring and summer fish but most hotels close to salmon rivers fill their deep-freezes for the winter. Poached, grilled or smoked Scotch salmon is unsurpassed.

Sea and *river trout, haddock, cod, plaice, turbot, lemon sole, flounder, lythe, saithe* and *mackerel* are all to be had but in severely diminished quantities.

Sweets and Puddings

Although Scotland often lacks sunshine and warmth, its raspberries and gooseberries, rowans and strawberries are exposed to a long ripening summer and have qualities not perhaps achieved in southern climes. But it is to puddings that we must turn in Scotland for something you won't find elsewhere in Britain:
Clootie Dumpling Apple, currants, raisins, mixed spice, treacle and suet boiled in a cloth or 'cloute' (pronounced *cloot*).
Cranachan A rich sweet of flavoured cream, or crowdie cheese, with toasted oatmeal.
Atholl Brose Not strictly a pudding, not strictly a drink, this combination of whisky, oatmeal, heather honey, cream and eggs is rich and heady.
Burnt Cream A Scots version of *crème brulée* — a rich egg custard covered with browned castor sugar.
Groset Fool Stewed gooseberries and elderflower heads whipped with cream.

Baking

The Scottish housewife is famous for her floury fingers and

whether she's making *Aberdeen butteries, bannocks (oatcakes),
girdle pancakes, shortbread, Dundee cake* or any number of tarts
and buns, all thoughts of slimming go out of the window.
Afternoon tea in Scotland can ruin your appetite for dinner!

Cheese

Although Scotland is not rich in dairy herds it nevertheless
produces a variety of cheeses both hard and soft.
Caboc is a double cream soft cheese rolled in pinhead oatmeal;
Crowdie, a fine cottage type cheese, is made from skimmed milk
curds and often sold mixed with cream and sometimes garlic.
Hard cheeses include *Dunlop,* a pale yellow cheese which was
originally made in Ayrshire; *Galloway,* a cheddar type cheese with
a rich flavour and creamy texture; *Arran,* a small round cheese
made at Kilmory creamery on the Isle of Arran; *Orkney* is made
on that northern island and *Gigha* comes from the Inner
Hebrides.

Take your cheese with oatmeal biscuits, or bannocks as they are
called.

Whisky Drinks

Whisky Mac. Two measures of whisky and one of green ginger wine.

Whisky Tom Collins. 5-6 dashes of lemon, a measure of whisky, some ice. Pour into a glass and add soda to taste.

Blood & Sand. Equal parts of whisky, cherry brandy, orange juice.

Stone Fence. Two ounces of whisky in a tall tumbler with ice — top up with cider.

Whisky Sour. Two measures of whisky, juice of half a lemon, ½ teaspoon sugar, white of egg. Shake with ice and serve with a dash of soda.

Highland Bitters. Grind 1¾ ounces gentian root, ½ ounce orange peel, 1 ounce coriander seed, ¼ ounce cinnamon. Add the mixture to a couple of bottles of Scotch and let it infuse for a fortnight.

Rob Roy. Two measures Scotch, one measure red vermouth, a dash of bitters.

Scotch Milk Punch. Shake 2 ounces of whisky and 6 ounces of milk with sugar and ice. Pour into glass and sprinkle with nutmeg.

Whisky Benedict. One measure whisky, one of Bénédictine, one of ginger ale.

Death in Paris. One measure of whisky, one of gin, one of pastis.

Whisky Toddy. Mix boiling water, sugar and whisky in a glass that won't crack — add a slice of lemon and a spoonful of honey.

Mac Horse's Neck. A measure of whisky, dash of lemon juice and Angostura topped up with ginger ale.

Het Pint. A drink for welcoming the New Year. Put four pints of ale in a saucepan, add a teaspoonful of grated nutmeg, simmer and stir in half a cup of sugar. Gradually beat in three eggs, add half a pint of whisky. Drink in large glasses.

Highland Coffee. Coffee and whisky, sweetened if desired and covered with cream.

Whisky Sling. Mix with ice, 1 teaspoonful of sugar, 2 teaspoonfuls of lemon juice, three measures of whisky and a dash of Angostura. Top up with soda water.

Auld Man's Milk. 'Beat the yolks and whites of half a dozen eggs separately. Add to the yolks sugar and a quart of milk or thin cream and to this about half a pint of whisky. The whipped whites are then united with this mixture and the whole is gently stirred in a punchbowl. Flavoured with nutmeg or lemon zest, this makes an admirable morning dram.'*Aeneas MacDonald.*

Caledonian Liquor. Drop an ounce of cinnamon oil on 2½ pounds of granulated sugar. Add eight pints of whisky, filter and bottle.

Summer Scotch. 1 glass of Scotch, 3 dashes of Crème de Menthe, add soda and ice.

LIQUEURS

There are several **whisky liqueurs** on the market, the oldest and best
known being **Drambuie,** a corruption of *An Dram Buidheach,* Gaelic for
the dram that satisfies. The recipe is said to have been given to a
Mackinnon of Strathaird in Skye by the fleeing Prince Charles Edward
Stuart in 1746; it is a selection of old Highland malts mixed with herbs
and honey. Other whisky liqueurs are **Lochan Ora** and **Glayva.**

APPENDIX 2

De Luxe Blends

Maker	*Blends*
George Ballantine & Son	Ballantine's
Barton Distilling (Scotland)	House of Stuart Royal (8 years old)
John Begg	Gold Cap
Arthur Bell & Sons	Bell's Deluxe 12 years old
	Royal Reserve 20 years old
	Specially Selected Blended Scotch Whisky
Benmore Distilleries	Benmore Special Reserve
Berry Bros. & Rudd	Berry's Best, St. James's 12 years old, Cutty 12 (12 years old)
James Buchanan & Co	Buchanan's, Royal Household
Bulloch Lade & Co	Old Rarity
Campbell & Clark	David Ross de Luxe
James Catto & Co	Catto's 12 year old
Chivas Bros	Chivas Regal, Royal Salute
John Crabbie & Co	Crabbie 12 years old
A. &. A. Crawford	Crawfords 'Five Star'
Peter Dawson	Old Curio
John Dewar & Sons	Ancestor, Ne Plus Ultra
The Distillers Agency	Highland Nectar
William Grant & Sons	Grant's Royal (over 12 years old)
John Haig & Co	Dimple
Hall & Bramley	Glen Ghoil
J. &. W. Hardie	The Antiquary
Hepburn & Ross	Red Hackle de Luxe,
	Red Hackle Reserve 12 years old
Hill Thomson & Co	Something Special
D. Johnston & Co (Laphroaig)	Islay Mist
Lang Bros	Lang's 12 years old de Luxe
William Lawson Distillers	William Lawson's 8 year old
Longman Distillers Co	Glen Eagle 8 years old,
	Longman 8 years old
D. & J. McCallum	McCallum's de Luxe
James McCreadie & Co	Mak Readie
Macdonald Greenlees	Old Parr, President
Macdonald & Muir	Highland Queen Grand 15
Chas. Mackinlay & Co	Legacy
Macleay Duff (Distillers)	Macleay Duff Antique
Duncan Macleod & Co	Glenfinnan Royal Liqueur
Robert Macnish & Co	Grand Macnish

James Martin & Co	Martin's de luxe,
	Martin's Fine & Rare
Stanley P. Morrison	Old Highland
James Munro & Son	King of Kings
Stewart & Son of Dundee	Cream of the Barley 8 year old,
	Queen's Own 8 year old
J. G. Stewart	Usher's de Luxe,
	Antique Jamie Stuart
Peter Thomson (Perth)	Old Perth De Luxe
John Walker & Sons	Johnnie Walker Black Label
Wauchope Moodie & Co	Criterion
White Horse Distillers	Logan
Wm. Whiteley & Co	King's Ransom
White and Mackay	Whyte and Mackay's Supreme,
	Whyte and Mackay's 21 years old

Who Owns What

The following companies own more than two distilleries (Grain in italics).

Arthur Bell
Blair Athol; Dufftown-Glenlivet; Inchgower; Pittyvaich-Glenlivet.

Joseph E. Seagram
Allta' Bhainne; Benriach; Caperdonich; Glen Grant-Glenlivet; The Glenlivet; Glen Keith-Glenlivet; Longmorn; Strathisla-Glenlivet; Braes of Glenlivet.

Distillers Company Limited (D.C.L.)
Aberfeldy; Aultmore; Balmenach; Banff; Benrinnes; Benromach; *Caledonian; Cambus; Cameronbridge;* Caol Ila; Cardow; Carsebridge; Clynelish; Coleburn; Convalmore; Cragganmore; Craigellachie; Dailuaine; Dallas Dhu; Dalwhinnie; Glen Albyn; Glendullan; Glen Elgin; Glenkinchie; Glenlochy; Glenlossie; Glen Mhor; Glentauchers; Glenury-Royal; Hillside; Imperial; Knockdhu; Lagavulin; Linkwood; Lochnagar; Mannochmore; Millburn; Mortlach; North Port; Oban; Ord; *Port Dundas;* Port Ellen; Rosebank; Royal Brackla; Speyburn; St. Magdalene; Talisker; Teaninich.

William Grant
Balvenie; *Girvan;* Glenfiddich; Ladyburn.

Highland Distilleries
Bunnahabhain; Glenglassaugh; Glenrothes-Glenlivet; Highland Park; Tamdhu.

International Distillers and Vintners (I.D.V.)
Auchroisk; Glen Spey; Knockando; Strathmill.

Invergordon Distillers
Bruichladdich; Ben Wyvis; Deanston; *Invergordon;* Tamnavulin; Tullibardine.

Inverhouse Distillers
Bladnoch; Glenflagler; *Moffat.*

Long John International
Glenugie; *Kinclaith;* Laphroaig; *Strathclyde;* Tormore.

Scottish Universal Investment Trust
Dalmore; Fettercairn; Tomintoul-Glenlivet.

Hiram Walker
Balblair; *Dumbarton;* Inverleven; Lomond; Glenburgie-Glenlivet; Glencadam; Glencraig; Miltonduff-Glenlivet; Pulteney; Scapa.

Glossary

Age. If a blender wishes to specify the age of the whiskies in a blend it must be the age of the *youngest* single component. The average age of a blend is much higher than that stated on the label.

Burnt Ale. See *Pot Ale*.

Butt. A cask containing 110 gallons.

Coffey Still. See *Patent Still*.

Congenerics. Malt whisky is full of trace elements, impurities if you like: aldehydes, esters, furfural and other compounds. These are the relatively unresearched indefinables that impart to malt whisky its unique and individual flavour.

Distillers Safe. See *Spirit Safe*.

Draff. The spent grain left in the mash-tun after the liquor has been drawn off. Roughly three-quarters of the grain used in whisky-making ends up as draff, which is processed into commercially profitable cattle food.

Dreg. The sediment left beneath the draining plates at the bottom of the mash-tun.

Gallonage. *Original* gallonage is the actual amount filled into cash; *regauge* gallonage is the amount which remains in the cask. See *Ullage*.

Feints. Impure spirits produced during the second distillation in the pot still process.

Fillings. New whisky.

Foreshots. The first raw runnings of the second distillation of the Low Wines. The foreshots give way to the potable spirit which in turn gives way to the last runnings or feints. When a distillery closes for its annual holiday the feints and foreshots from the last distillation are stored and then added to the first low wines of the succeeding season.

Fusel Oil. A mixture of the higher alcohols with water and spirit.

Gill. In England and Wales whisky is usually sold in one-sixth gills (five-sixths of a fluid ounce). In Scotland it is usually a one-fifth measure (1 fluid ounce).

Grain Spirit. See *Patent Still*.

Green Malt. Undried malted barley.

Grist. Ground malted barley.

Hogshead. Cask containing 55-56 gallons.

Kiln. The pagoda-roofed building in which the green malt is spread on perforated iron sheets to be heat-dried and peated. The old-style distillery malt barns have now largely been replaced by centralised maltings, where the barley is germinated in mechanical drums known as *Saladin boxes*. It is a more labour-saving, efficient and economic method but far less picturesque.

Low Wines. The product of the first distillation of the wash. The spirits are weak and impure and form the raw material of the second distillation in the spirit still.

Lyne Arm. The wide diameter pipe which connects the head of the still to the condensing unit. The angle of the arm plays a vital part in the quality of the spirit produced. One eminent distiller told me with a deadpan face that he knew of a distillery where the lyne arm was on a pulley: 'they adjust the angle depending on what sort of whisky the customer wants, heavy or light.' I still don't know whether he was pulling my leg or being frank and indiscreet.

Mashing. The infusion of cereal with hot water.

Mash-tun. The vessel in which the mashing process takes place.

Patent Still. Sometimes known as the *Coffey Still* after its inventor, Aeneas Coffey. it consists of two colums, an analyser and a rectifier in which steam heat vapourises alcohol from the wash. The process is more economic than pot distillation, being more canny with ingredients, fuel and water — the vapours heat the wash and the wash condenses the vapours. The grain spirit produced lacks the *congenerics* found in malt whisky: it is milder and generally reaches maturity in 3-5 years.

Pot Still. A large onion or pear-shaped copper vessel. The distillation process requires two stills: a wash still in which the fermented wash is heated until all the alcohol is driven off and a spirit still in which the final potable spirit is isolated.

Proof Spirit. Spirit is proof when at a temperature of 11°C (51°F) it weighs 12/13th of a volume of distilled water equal to the volume in spirits.

Rummager. Four rotating arms which control a copper chain mesh dragged round the bottom of the wash still to prevent the wash from sticking to the bottom and burning. Unnecessary in steam-heated stills.

Shiel. The wooden shovel used to turn the germinating barley on the floor of the malt barn.

Single Whisky. The product of one distillery, grain or malt.

Spent Lees. The residue left in the spirit still after the foreshots, potable spirits and feints have been distilled.

Spirit Safe or *Distillers Safe*. The conspicuously-padlocked brass coffin with glass sides which receives the low wines. Thermometers, hydrometers and an educated eye enable the stillman to decide when the runnings become potable.

Spirit Still. See *Pot Still*.

Steeps. Tanks normally holding about half a ton of barley in which the grain is soaked before malting.

Tubular Condenser. The modern replacement for the traditional worm.

Ullage. Spirit lost by evaporation during maturation. In a normal year about 12 million proof gallons vanish into the air above Scotland.

Underback. The worts receiver.

Vatting. The mixing of single whiskies.

Wash Still. See *Pot Still*.

Washback. The vat in which the wort with added yeast begins its fermenting process. They vary in capacity from a thousand to ten thousand gallons.

Worm. A coiled copper tube, cooled by running water, through whose diminishing diameter the alcoholic vapours condense.

Wort. The liquid containing all the sugars of the malt which is drawn off after the malt has been mashed with warm water. After cooling, the wort is passed to the fermenting vats.

Zymase. This and *maltose* are the two yeast enzymes which between them convert the maltose of the mash into alcoholic and carbon dioxide.

Further Reading

Barnard, Alfred. *The Whisky Distilleries of the United Kingdom.* Harper, 1887.
Alfred Barnard went by boat, train and carriage to visit every distillery in Great Britain and his monumental work creates a vivid picture of Scotland in the time when whisky was booming. The period illustrations that decorate this book are drawn from Barnard's pages.

Brander, Michael. *A Guide to Scotch Whisky.* Johnston & Bacon, 1974.
A good little paperback, full of information.

Brander, Michael. *The Original Scotch.* Hutchinson, 1974.
A history of Scotch whisky sponsored by The Glenlivet Distillers; it is more than a tribute to George Smith, however, being rich in social, economic and historical detail from the earliest days of distilling.

Daiches, David. *Scotch Whisky. Its Past and Present.* Andre Deutch, 1969.
A highly personal but objective account of whisky; how it is made and how it tastes. Revised in 1978.

Gunn, Neil M. *Whisky and Scotland.* Routledge, 1935.
Neil Gunn, Exciseman and author, produced this very affectionate and dedicated tribute to malt whisky after 30 years working in distilleries. The book was reissued as a paperback in 1977.

House, Jack. *Pride of Perth.* Hutchinson Benham, 1976.

Laver, James. *The House of Haig.* 1958.
The official house histories of Bell and Haig.

Lockhart, Sir Robert Bruce. *Scotch.* Putnam, 1959.
The author spent his boyhood on Speyside and his book is part history, part nostalgia but full of good things.

MacDonald, Aeneas. *Whisky.* The Porpoise Press, 1930.
A splendid and rumbustious polemic in praise of malt.

McDowall, R. J. S. *The Whiskies of Scotland.* John Murray, 1967.
A practical, informed and useful survey of the whisky scene.

Robb, J. Marshall. *Scotch Whisky.* W. & R. Chambers, 1950.
Gobbets and snippets of information about whisky; light and readable.

Ross, James. *Whisky.* Routledge & Kegan Paul, 1970.
The late James Ross was a Skyeman and Gaelic scholar and this is the only book I know which reflects the part that *uisge beatha* played in the Gaelic-speaking west.

Sillett, S. W. *Illicit Scotch.* Beaver Books. Aberdeen, 1965.
Smugglers' tales old and new written by an Exciseman.

Wilson, Ross. *Scotch Made Easy.* Hutchinson, 1959; *Scotch.* Constable,

1970; *Scotch, Its History and Romance.* David & Charles, 1973.
Few writers know more about whisky than Ross Wilson; he is authoritative and comprehensive.

Maps

The *Scotch Whisky Association,* Half Moon Street, London W1, produces a wall map of Scotland showing the distilleries, with a numbered list of them that corresponds to the numbering used for the maps in this book. *Johnston & Bacon,* Edinburgh, publish a **Whisky Map of Scotland,** which includes useful information on the distilling process. For touring, the maps produced by *Bartholomew* (1:100,000) and the *Ordnance Survey* (1:50,000) have all the necessary local detail.

Index